BUSINESS PATTERN SCIENCE

PATTERN SCIENCE

Why Chaos Isn't Random —
and What to Do About It

Troy Fazakerley

Founder, Business Alchemy Australia Pty Ltd

The Defining Practice of Business Pattern Architecture

Pattern Science: Why Chaos Isn't Random and What to Do About It

Published by Business Alchemy Australia Pty Ltd

Queensland, Australia

businessalchemy.au | info@businessalchemy.au

First Edition — 2026

Printed in Australia

For Renae.

Who understood the human patterns

while I was still mapping the structural ones.

For my Daughters.

Who inspire me everyday.

And for every founder who called it chaos

when it was always a pattern waiting to be seen.

Contents

Preface

A Note Before We Begin

I didn't set out to write a book about chaos.

I set out to understand why some businesses transform and others regress. Why the same intervention lands differently in two businesses of identical size, sector, and ambition. Why a strategy that should work — based on every framework I'd studied and every consultant I'd observed — simply doesn't hold.

I spent two decades looking for the answer in the usual places. Better strategy. Stronger leadership. Improved systems. And I found the same result every time: the improvement held for a season, and then something deeper reasserted itself, pulling the business back toward its original state. The pattern — the invisible architecture beneath the visible operations — remained unchanged.

That's when the question shifted. Instead of asking "what should we change," I started asking: "what is generating the current state?" Not what's wrong at the surface. What structural pattern is producing the surface?

That question changed everything.

"Chaos isn't random. It's a pattern. And patterns can be changed."

This book is the result of two decades of asking that question in real businesses under real pressure. It is not a theoretical framework built in an office. Every concept in here has been stress-tested in the field — in construction companies, engineering firms, healthcare businesses, and renewable energy operations. In businesses where the stakes were real, the margins were visible, and the patterns kept asserting themselves regardless of what the whiteboard said.

It introduces a new management discipline: Pattern Science™. Not a new consulting approach. Not a new leadership model. A science — with a defined diagnostic architecture, a formally documented interpretation logic, and a sequenced intervention methodology that addresses causes, not symptoms.

Business Alchemy™ is its practice. This book is its foundation.

A word about structure. This book moves in three phases. It begins where your experience begins — in the chaos, the frustration, the sense that something beneath the surface is working against you. It then earns the right to go deeper — into the science, the architecture, the five patterns and their constraint hierarchy. And it closes with the practical intelligence you need to act: how to diagnose your patterns, how to correct them in sequence, and how to build the structural momentum that makes growth feel inevitable rather than exhausting.

Read it all the way through once before you begin applying it. The sequence matters. That's the first lesson of Pattern Science.

Troy Fazakerley

Queensland, Australia — 2026

Part One
The Problem

"The definition of insanity is doing the same thing over and over and expecting different results."

— Often attributed to Albert Einstein

Chapter 1

Chaos Has a Structure

Why your business feels broken when nothing is technically wrong

There is a particular kind of exhaustion that founder-led businesses produce. It is not the exhaustion of hard work, though the work is hard. It is the exhaustion of effort that doesn't compound. Of progress that doesn't hold. Of problems that keep returning in slightly different forms no matter what you do about them.

You have hired the right people. You have invested in the systems. You have attended the strategy days, engaged the consultants, read the books. And yet the business feels like it is fighting against itself — generating friction in places that should be frictionless, producing inconsistency in areas where you have built processes specifically to ensure consistency.

Most founders reach a point where they stop asking "what can I fix?" and start asking a darker question: "Is this just what running a business feels like?"

It isn't. But the reason it feels this way is real, and it has nothing to do with your strategy, your team, or your effort.

The Real Source of Business Chaos

Your business is not chaotic because of bad luck, bad hiring, or bad strategy. It is chaotic because of patterns.

A pattern, in the context of this book, is not a trend or a habit. It is something more fundamental: a self-reinforcing structural architecture — a recurring configuration of structural conditions, behavioural responses, and outcome regularities that collectively determine how your business performs, scales, and sustains itself over time.

Patterns are not events. Events happen and pass. Patterns persist. They reassert themselves. They shape behaviour so deeply that the people inside the system stop noticing them — the dysfunction becomes the new normal, and the normal becomes invisible.

This is why tactics fail. Not because the tactics are wrong. Because tactics are applied at the surface of a system whose underlying architecture is generating a different result. You can hire a better operations manager, but if the Ownership pattern of your business hasn't changed, the new manager will eventually behave the way every manager before them did — because the system generates that behaviour regardless of who occupies the role.

"Fix the symptom and the pattern generates a new one. Fix the pattern and the symptoms stop appearing."

— Pattern Science™ — First Principle

Science Foundation

Ludwig von Bertalanffy's General Systems Theory (1968) established that systems behave as integrated wholes — that dysfunction in one subsystem propagates across the entire structure in predictable ways. Gregory Bateson extended this to pattern theory: the "pattern that connects" is not located in individual elements but in the relationships between them. Pattern Science™ applies this systems logic directly to the architecture of organisations.

The Division That Needed to Shrink

A story from the field.

A company called me in with a clear brief: their field installation and maintenance division — around $18 million in revenue — was losing money every month and no one could explain why. They needed someone on the ground to find out.

When I arrived, the local Managing Director had a clear view of the problem: it was the team. Wrong people, wrong attitude, wrong execution. He'd been saying it for months.

I spent the first week not looking at the team. I looked at the financials. And I found the first structural problem immediately: the MD was the only person in the organisation who could see the financial data. His managers — the people running the field operations, managing the crews, quoting the work — had no visibility of their own performance. They didn't know whether the jobs they were delivering were profitable. They couldn't have taken ownership of the numbers even if they'd wanted to, because the numbers weren't theirs to see.

The team wasn't underperforming. They were operating blind.

When I put the financial picture in front of the leadership team — showed them the margin by project type, the cost blowouts by crew, the work that was actively losing money every time it was quoted — the room went quiet. Not because they were shocked. Because they recognised it. They had suspected it. They just hadn't been trusted with the evidence.

We built the Ownership architecture around the data. Scorecards. Decision ladders. Weekly numbers reviews where each manager reported on their own margin performance. For the first time, the people closest to the work owned the outcomes of the work.

Then we looked at the revenue. The business was doing too much of the wrong work. When we ran the Margin Diagnostic, the picture was unambiguous. The recommendation wasn't popular initially: scale back. Exit the low-margin contracts. Rebuild around the work that actually made money. Go from $18 million to $10 million in revenue — intentionally — in order to stop the bleeding and build a profitable foundation.

The division went from losing money at $18 million to generating healthy margin at $10 million. Less revenue. More profit. A leadership team that finally knew their numbers, owned their results, and made decisions without waiting for permission.

The MD left during the process. I was asked to lead the turnaround through to completion.

The team that had been blamed was never the problem. They were the symptom of an Ownership pattern that kept them powerless, a Value pattern that kept them unprofitable, and a Clarity pattern that kept them in the dark about both.

Fix the pattern. The team fixes itself.

What Makes Patterns Invisible

The most dangerous property of a business pattern is that it becomes invisible to the people living inside it. Psychologists call this normalisation of dysfunction — the process by which abnormal conditions are gradually recategorised as simply "how things are."

In business, this manifests in specific ways. Founders stop noticing the pattern because they have adapted to working within it. They have developed workarounds, compensations, and routines specifically designed to manage around the structural constraint rather than address it. Over time, the compensation becomes the system, and the underlying constraint becomes completely invisible.

This is why external diagnosis matters. Not because outsiders are smarter, but because they haven't adapted. They can still see the pattern because they haven't yet learned to look past it.

The Pattern Insight

The longer you have operated inside a business pattern, the less visible it becomes. The founder who calls their business "chaotic" is usually describing the symptom of a pattern they have adapted around so completely they can no longer see it directly. The first diagnostic act of Pattern Science is to make the invisible visible.

The Five Patterns That Govern Everything

Through twenty years of diagnostic work across hundreds of founder-led businesses, one architectural truth has emerged with striking consistency: every organisational outcome — every performance result, every cultural dynamic, every margin, every growth rate — traces back to one or more of five structural patterns operating beneath the surface of the business.

These are not management functions. They are not departments or disciplines. They are the five interdependent patterns that form the complete architecture of how a business performs:

- **Ownership** — the pattern governing accountability, decision quality, and the distribution of leadership authority

- **Clarity** — the pattern governing strategic direction, priority architecture, and the operational translation of where the business is going
- **Rhythm** — the pattern governing execution cadence, performance consistency, and the predictable operating system that converts strategy into daily output
- **Flow** — the pattern governing team cohesion, leadership communication, and the cultural conditions that allow talent to perform sustainably
- **Value** — the pattern governing commercial leverage, margin architecture, and enterprise value creation

These five patterns are not independent. They are interdependent in a specific, directional way — upstream patterns are structural prerequisites for downstream pattern performance. Ownership governs Clarity. Clarity governs Rhythm. Rhythm governs Flow. Flow governs Value.

This interdependency is not incidental. It is the central architectural insight of Pattern Science, and it is what distinguishes this methodology from every other advisory framework currently operating in the market. Most frameworks treat these domains as parallel work streams to be addressed simultaneously. Pattern Science treats them as a constraint hierarchy — where the order of correction is as important as the correction itself.

We will spend an entire part of this book on each pattern. But first, we need to understand the second foundational principle of Pattern Science: why the lowest-performing area is almost never where you should begin.

Chapter Summary

- Business chaos is not random. It is the visible symptom of invisible structural patterns operating beneath the surface of every organisation.
- Patterns are self-reinforcing architectural configurations that generate consistent outcomes regardless of the tactics or people applied on top of them.
- Tactics fail not because they are wrong, but because they address symptoms rather than the patterns generating them.
- Five interdependent patterns govern the complete architecture of business performance: Ownership, Clarity, Rhythm, Flow, and Value.
- The order in which patterns are addressed is as important as the correction itself.

Chapter 2

The Constraint That Governs Everything

Why fixing the wrong thing first guarantees regression

There is a principle in physics so simple it seems obvious and so consequential it changes everything: in any system, one constraint governs total throughput more than all other factors combined.

Strengthen any part of the system that is not the primary constraint, and total throughput does not improve. The bottleneck simply moves. The system finds a new way to express the same limitation. And the improvement you thought you had made quietly disappears.

Eliyahu Goldratt demonstrated this in manufacturing environments in 1984, in a book called The Goal, that became one of the most influential management texts of the twentieth century. The insight was initially controversial, then widely accepted, then largely misapplied — because the manufacturing metaphor was never properly translated into the organisational context where it is most needed.

Pattern Science makes that translation explicit. The five business patterns operate in a constraint hierarchy. And in that hierarchy, one pattern is almost always the primary constraint — the pattern whose weakness is most actively suppressing the performance of the patterns that depend on it.

The Most Counterintuitive Principle in Business

Here is the principle that most consultants violate and most business owners resist: the lowest-scoring pattern in your business is almost never the primary constraint.

Read that again, because it contradicts almost everything you've been told about business improvement.

If your Flow scores are low — if your team has communication problems, culture friction, or engagement issues — your first instinct is to address Flow. Run a team workshop. Engage a leadership coach. Address the interpersonal dynamics that are producing the friction. This instinct is rational. And it is almost always wrong.

Low Flow scores are almost always the downstream symptom of an upstream pattern deficiency. The team communication is breaking down because the execution environment is chaotic (Rhythm problem). The execution environment is chaotic because the strategic direction keeps changing (Clarity problem). The strategic direction keeps changing because no one in the leadership team genuinely owns the strategy except the founder (Ownership problem).

Fix Flow directly, and you get a temporary improvement followed by regression. The upstream constraints remain active, and they continue generating the conditions that suppress Flow. Within ninety days, the culture workshop has been forgotten and the friction has returned — slightly mutated but structurally identical.

"Every consultant who has ever been called back to fix the same problem they fixed eighteen months ago made the same error: they addressed the symptom and left the constraint intact."

The Three States of Pattern Dysfunction

Before you can identify your primary constraint, you need to understand that pattern dysfunction presents in three fundamentally different states — and each state requires a completely different response.

This is one of the most consequential distinctions in Pattern Science, and it is one that almost no other framework makes explicit.

State One: Absent

The pattern's structural infrastructure does not exist. There are no accountability mechanisms, no strategic documentation, no execution cadence — the architecture has never been built. This is the state of a young or fast-growing business that has outpaced its own structure. Things work because of heroic individual effort and founder presence, not because of structural design.

Absent patterns need building from scratch. They require foundational work — the deliberate construction of structural infrastructure that doesn't yet exist.

State Two: Misaligned

The pattern's infrastructure exists but is incorrectly configured — strategy not connected to execution, accountability not connected to outcomes, rhythm not connected to priorities. The business has structure but the structure doesn't produce results. Leaders frequently say: "We have the system but it doesn't work."

Misaligned patterns need correction and realignment. The architecture exists; it needs reconfiguring to the correct operational specification.

State Three: Suppressed

The pattern's infrastructure exists and is correctly configured, but its performance is artificially depressed by an upstream pattern deficiency. The pattern cannot express its potential because a dependency is unmet. This is the state of the business whose Flow is strong in theory but keeps breaking down in practice — not because the team culture is wrong, but because the Rhythm environment in which the team operates is chaotic.

Suppressed patterns need upstream correction first — not direct intervention. Direct intervention on a suppressed pattern produces temporary improvement followed by rapid regression, because the structural suppressor remains active. The pattern is being pushed down by something above it in the hierarchy.

! Critical Distinction

The most dangerous diagnostic error in business advisory is treating a suppressed pattern as absent or misaligned. Absent patterns need building. Misaligned patterns need reconfiguring. Suppressed patterns need upstream correction first. Direct intervention on a suppressed pattern is the primary cause of the "six-month regression" that characterises most consulting engagements that fail to hold.

The Four Suppression Archetypes

Pattern Science has identified four recurring suppression archetypes — configurations of upstream constraint that appear consistently across different industries, business models, and growth stages. Learning to recognise these archetypes is one of the most practically valuable skills a business leader can develop, because they allow you to hear a client's description of their business and immediately map it to its structural root.

Archetype One: The Founder Bottleneck

Ownership to Clarity Suppression

The most common suppression archetype in founder-led businesses below $10 million in revenue. The Ownership pattern structural coherence is compromised — the founder is the accountability system, decisions flow through one person, and the leadership team has no authentic ownership of outcomes. This suppresses Clarity because the strategic direction is held in the founder's head and interpreted differently by every leader in the absence of structural documentation and clear ownership.

The business has strategy documents but no one can articulate the strategy. Leadership team meetings produce agreement but not alignment. Execution inconsistency is blamed on the team's capability. It is actually a structural accountability deficit.

From the Field

Founder language: "I end up doing it myself in the end." "My managers are great at their jobs but they won't make decisions." "I can't trust anyone else to do it to my standard." Every one of these sentences describes a suppressed Clarity pattern generated by an Ownership structural deficit.

Archetype Two: Strategic Chaos

Clarity to Rhythm Suppression

The second most common archetype, typically seen in businesses that have resolved Ownership but not yet operationalised strategy. Clarity is absent or misaligned — direction changes frequently, priorities are numerous and competing, strategy is aspirational rather than operational. This suppresses Rhythm because execution cadence cannot organise around a moving or unclear strategic signal.

The business has excellent operational people who cannot execute consistently. Priority is a word that has lost meaning. Every week brings new urgent imperatives that override last week's commitments.

From the Field

Founder language: "Everyone is pulling in slightly different directions." "We keep saying yes to things that don't fit our strategy." "Our three-year plan is in my head."

Archetype Three: Cultural Friction

Rhythm to Flow Suppression

A pattern typically seen in businesses experiencing rapid growth or organisational transition. Rhythm structural coherence has degraded — meeting cadences are inconsistent, accountability rhythms are skipped under pressure, execution is reactive. This suppresses Flow because interpersonal trust and collaborative cohesion require operational predictability to sustain.

The team describes communication problems and cultural deterioration. Leadership identifies this as a culture problem. It is a Rhythm deficit creating the conditions for Flow deterioration.

From the Field

An electrical services company called me in to fix the culture in their dispatch team. Relations between dispatch and the field crews had broken down. Client trust was eroding. They had tried pizza Fridays and ergonomic chairs. Nothing had changed. When I sat with each team separately, both sides were accurately describing the same structural failure from opposite sides of it. The founders were absent strategically — no defined service delivery model, no agreed handoff process, no shared understanding of what a successfully completed job looked like end to end. This was not a culture problem. It was a Clarity and Rhythm problem wearing culture's clothes. I mapped the service delivery model end to end, simplified the daily operating goals to reduce cognitive load, and gave every person in the business a clear, specific picture of their part. When people understand their role specifically — not generally — the blame stops. Not because the culture improved. Because the structural ambiguity that was generating the conflict was gone.

Archetype Four: Margin Leakage

Flow to Value Suppression

Typically seen in businesses with strong revenue but deteriorating margins. Flow is disrupted — leadership cohesion is low, internal friction is high, talent is underutilised or misaligned. This suppresses Value because commercial leverage requires a functioning leadership team to identify, price, and protect margin.

Revenue is adequate but margins are declining. Client relationships are strained. The business is busy but not profitable. This is identified as a pricing or sales problem. It is a Flow problem suppressing Value architecture.

From the Field

Founder language: "We're busy but not making money." "We keep taking on clients that drain us." "Our best revenue comes from a small number of clients."

The Constraint Hierarchy: Primary, Secondary, Tertiary

Once you have identified the suppression archetype operating in your business, the next step is to establish the constraint hierarchy — which pattern to address first, which second, and which to leave alone because it is a tertiary symptom that will resolve naturally once the upstream constraints are corrected.

The rules are clear:

- The primary constraint is the pattern whose weakness most suppresses the structural coherence of downstream patterns. Correcting this unlocks the greatest total system improvement. It is addressed first and exclusively until its structural coherence is established.
- The secondary constraint is a pattern that is genuinely underperforming but not currently suppressing others — or whose suppression will be exposed once the primary constraint is corrected. It begins to be addressed in parallel with primary constraint consolidation.
- The tertiary constraint is a pattern suppressed by the primary or secondary constraint. Its low score is a downstream effect, not a root cause. Do not address it directly. Monitor for natural improvement as upstream constraints are corrected.

This is the logic that the Interpretation Doctrine™ formalises — the governing document of Pattern Science that determines exactly how diagnostic data is read, how the constraint hierarchy is established, and what intervention sequence is required. We will return to it in depth when we reach the diagnostic chapters.

For now, the critical insight is this: the sequence of intervention is not a preference. It is a structural necessity. Correcting patterns out of sequence does not produce suboptimal results. It produces the most dangerous outcome in business transformation: a false recovery signal — the appearance of improvement that masks the continued operation of the primary constraint.

Chapter Summary

- In any system, one constraint governs total throughput more than all other factors combined. Strengthening non-constraints produces no improvement in total system output.
- The lowest-performing pattern in your business is almost never the primary constraint. It is almost always a suppressed downstream effect of an upstream structural deficit.
- Pattern dysfunction presents in three states — Absent, Misaligned, and Suppressed — each requiring a completely different intervention response.
- Four suppression archetypes account for the majority of constraint patterns in founder-led businesses: Founder Bottleneck, Strategic Chaos, Cultural Friction, and Margin Leakage.
- The sequence of intervention is not a preference — it is a structural necessity. Correcting patterns out of sequence produces false recovery signals that mask the continued operation of the primary constraint.

Chapter 3

Why Everything You've Tried Hasn't Held

The five reasons smart interventions produce temporary results

If you have been running a business for more than five years, you have almost certainly experienced the following: a significant investment — of money, time, or leadership energy — in an intervention that produced visible results for a period of three to nine months, then quietly reversed.

The new CRM that cleaned up the pipeline management process, then gradually stopped being used as the team reverted to spreadsheets and phone calls. The leadership program that transformed the culture conversation, then lost momentum as the business pressures of the next quarter consumed the available energy. The consultant who restructured the operations, then watched as the restructured operations drifted back to their original configuration within twelve months.

This is not a failure of willpower. It is not a failure of the intervention. It is the predictable consequence of treating a pattern problem as a process problem.

The Five Failure Modes of Business Intervention

Twenty years of diagnostic work has produced a clear picture of why business interventions fail to hold. There are five distinct failure modes, and each one has a structural explanation.

Failure Mode One: Symptom Intervention

The intervention addresses the visible symptom rather than the generating pattern. This is the most common failure mode and the hardest to avoid, because symptoms are highly visible and emotionally compelling. The client presents with a cultural problem; the intervention addresses culture. The client presents with an execution problem; the intervention addresses execution.

The symptom is resolved. The pattern that generated the symptom is untouched. Within six months, the pattern has generated a new symptom — sometimes identical to the first, sometimes mutated into a slightly different form that triggers a new round of interventions.

From the Field

Two founders had built a construction business to $10 million in three years. Rapid growth is genuinely impressive — and genuinely destructive if the structural foundation doesn't keep up. By the time I sat with them, they were running on adrenaline and instinct, every week fighting problems that hadn't existed the week before. When the suppression map came back I presented it the way I always do — not as a report card but as a structural picture. Here is what is generating what. Here is why the thing you keep trying to fix keeps coming back. The room went quiet. Then one of the founders leaned forward and said: 'Finally. We will fix this properly so we can scale.' Not relief that someone had identified the problem. Relief that someone had identified the sequence. They had known something was fundamentally wrong. What they hadn't had was a structural explanation for why their fixes weren't holding.

Failure Mode Two: Sequencing Error

The intervention addresses a genuine pattern problem, but in the wrong order. Flow is addressed before Rhythm is established. Value is addressed before Ownership is corrected. The intervention is structurally sound in isolation — but it is being applied to a suppressed pattern, which means it is addressing an effect while leaving the cause intact.

This produces the most insidious failure mode of all: the intervention works, demonstrates results, and is considered successful — until the suppressing upstream constraint eventually destabilises it. The client concludes the methodology failed. The methodology was never the problem.

Failure Mode Three: Behavioural Before Structural

The intervention addresses behavioural change without first establishing the structural conditions that make the behavioural change sustainable. Leadership coaching is the most common example. Coaching a founder on delegation behaviour when no accountability architecture, decision ladder, or scorecard system exists is the equivalent of coaching someone to run faster on a surface that actively generates mud. The behaviour changes temporarily. The structure generates the old behaviour again.

Science Foundation

Kurt Lewin's Field Theory — B = f(P,E), that behaviour is a function of the person and the environment — establishes the foundational principle. Environments shape behaviour more powerfully than individual attributes. Structural conditions are the environment. Behavioural coaching without structural correction changes the person while leaving the environment intact. The environment wins.

Failure Mode Four: Parallel Implementation

The intervention attempts to address multiple patterns simultaneously, on the assumption that addressing all problems at once is more efficient than sequencing them. This is the architectural assumption that most major consulting frameworks make — and it is incorrect for a specific, theoretically grounded reason.

Simultaneous multi-pattern restructuring creates organisational instability and generates false recovery signals. When you attempt to change Ownership, Clarity, Rhythm, Flow, and Value at the same time, you create a period of maximum structural disruption in which the organisation loses its existing stabilising patterns before new ones are established. In this window, performance typically deteriorates before it improves. Most organisations abandon the transformation during this deterioration, concluding that the methodology isn't working.

Sequenced correction avoids this entirely. Each pattern is stabilised before the next is addressed. The organisation retains structural coherence throughout the transformation process.

Failure Mode Five: Diagnosis Without Doctrine

The intervention uses a diagnostic tool to identify problems but has no governing logic for interpreting the diagnostic data or determining the correct intervention sequence. The practitioner or founder sees a low score, identifies it as the problem, and designs an intervention around it — without completing the suppression analysis that would reveal whether the low score is a primary constraint or a downstream symptom.

This is why the Interpretation Doctrine™ exists. It is not a consulting preference or a methodology style. It is the formal governance document that prevents the five failure modes by mandating a specific diagnostic and sequencing logic before any intervention is recommended.

> ***"The consultant who produces durable results and the one who produces temporary results are not separated by intelligence, experience, or framework quality. They are separated by whether they have a doctrine for reading and sequencing their diagnostic data."***

The Regime of Improvement vs. The Regime of Transformation

This distinction is one of the most practically important in Pattern Science.

A regime of improvement is a business operating model in which performance is maintained and incrementally enhanced through ongoing tactical attention. Processes are refined. People are developed. Systems are upgraded. The business gets measurably better year over year, but its underlying pattern architecture remains unchanged. This is the dominant mode of operation in most well-run businesses, and there is nothing wrong with it — provided the pattern architecture is already sound.

A regime of transformation is required when the underlying pattern architecture is generating structural constraints that a regime of improvement cannot overcome. In a transformation regime, the business must accept temporary disruption of its current stabilising patterns in order to establish a new structural foundation from which it can compound.

Most businesses that feel chronically stuck are stuck not because they are poorly run but because they are applying an improvement regime to a situation that requires transformation. They are getting incrementally better at working inside a pattern that is structurally incapable of generating the outcomes they need.

Pattern Science is a transformation discipline. It does not make businesses incrementally better. It changes the structural architecture from which all subsequent improvement compounds.

Chapter Summary

- Business interventions fail to hold for five specific structural reasons: symptom intervention, sequencing error, behavioural before structural, parallel implementation, and diagnosis without doctrine.
- Environments shape behaviour more powerfully than individual attributes. Structural correction must precede behavioural development.
- Simultaneous multi-pattern restructuring creates organisational instability. Sequenced correction maintains structural coherence throughout transformation.
- Most stuck businesses are applying an improvement regime to a situation that requires structural transformation.
- Pattern Science is a transformation discipline — it changes the structural architecture from which all subsequent improvement compounds.

Part Two
The Science

"In physics, momentum is the product of mass and velocity. In business, momentum is the product of capacity and rhythm."

— Troy Fazakerley

Chapter 4

Pattern Science™

The new management discipline and what makes it different

Every generation of management thinking introduces a new frame for understanding why some businesses perform and others don't.

Frederick Taylor gave us scientific management — the idea that work could be optimised through time and motion studies, standardised processes, and systematic measurement. Peter Drucker gave us management by objectives — the idea that organisations perform when individuals are aligned to clear goals and held accountable for outcomes. W. Edwards Deming gave us quality management — the idea that performance is a function of system design rather than individual effort. Michael Porter gave us competitive strategy — the idea that sustainable advantage comes from deliberate positioning within an industry structure.

Each of these frameworks was correct within its domain. Each was also incomplete — because each addressed a layer of organisational performance while leaving the underlying structural pattern architecture unaddressed.

Pattern Science™ is the discipline that addresses what they left behind.

What Pattern Science Is

Pattern Science is the management discipline of identifying, measuring, and correcting the structural patterns governing how organisations perform, scale, and generate enterprise value.

It is built on three theoretical pillars, each drawn from established bodies of scientific research:

- General Systems Theory: organisations are not collections of independent functions but integrated systems in which patterns in one subsystem propagate across all others in predictable ways
- Theory of Constraints: in any system with a goal, one constraint limits total system throughput more than all other factors combined, and strengthening non-constraints produces no improvement in total output
- Behavioural Science: structural conditions shape behaviour more powerfully than individual attributes, and durable behavioural change requires structural correction as its foundation

The intersection of these three pillars produces the core insight of Pattern Science: business performance is not governed by strategy, talent, or systems in isolation. It is governed by five interdependent structural patterns operating in a constraint hierarchy — and durable transformation only occurs when those patterns are identified, sequenced, and corrected from the constraint outward.

> ***"Business Pattern Science is the first management discipline to treat the sequence of correction as a structural necessity rather than a practitioner preference."***
>
> *— Pattern Science™ — Theoretical Foundation Document*

The Four Research Streams That Built the Discipline

Research Stream One: General Systems Theory

Ludwig von Bertalanffy's General Systems Theory (1968) established that systems exhibit emergent properties — behaviours that arise from the interaction of parts and cannot be predicted from the parts in isolation. Gregory Bateson extended this to pattern theory: the pattern that connects is not located in individual elements but in their relationships. Peter Senge's The Fifth Discipline (1990) brought systems thinking into management practice.

Pattern Science applies these insights directly: the five patterns are not separate management domains but an integrated system. Their interdependency is not incidental but structural, and interventions that ignore this interdependency will consistently produce suboptimal results.

Research Stream Two: Theory of Constraints

Eliyahu Goldratt's Theory of Constraints (The Goal, 1984) demonstrated in manufacturing contexts that throughput is governed by the weakest link — the constraint — and that improvements to non-constraints shift the bottleneck but do not increase overall system output.

Pattern Science extends this logic from manufacturing throughput to organisational pattern architecture. The constraint is not the weakest function but the pattern whose weakness most suppresses the structural coherence of the patterns that depend on it. The Interpretation Doctrine™ is the operational expression of Goldratt's Five Focusing Steps — Identify, Exploit, Subordinate, Elevate, Repeat — applied to the five-pattern architecture of founder-led businesses.

Research Stream Three: Behavioural Psychology

Edward Deci and Richard Ryan's Self-Determination Theory (1985) established that human motivation and sustained behavioural engagement require three psychological conditions: Autonomy, Competence, and Relatedness. These conditions map directly to the Ownership, Clarity, and Flow patterns respectively.

Teresa Amabile and Steven Kramer's The Progress Principle (2011) established through extensive diary study research that the single most powerful driver of positive inner work life is making progress in meaningful work — not recognition, not leadership inspiration, not team events. Progress is the primary fuel of sustained motivation. Pattern Science frames this finding structurally: structural momentum is the mechanism through which progress is made consistently and predictably. Structure generates progress; progress generates motivation; motivation reinforces structure.

Research Stream Four: Cognitive Psychology

John Sweller's Cognitive Load Theory (1988) provides the theoretical basis for the Clarity pattern — specifically, why organisational complexity and strategic ambiguity produce decision quality degradation and execution failure. When cognitive load exceeds working memory capacity, decision-making becomes reactive rather than strategic. The Clarity playbook actions — Critical Few priorities, Opportunity Filter, Role Clarity documents — are directly derived from Cognitive Load Theory's prescription for reducing extraneous cognitive load in complex systems.

Kurt Lewin's Field Theory — B = f(P,E), that behaviour is a function of the person and the environment — provides the foundational argument for the structural primacy principle: environments shape behaviour more powerfully than individual attributes. Lewin's Unfreeze-Change-Refreeze change model provides the theoretical basis for the 90-Day Alchemy Cycle's three-phase structure.

What Makes Pattern Science Different From the Frameworks You've Already Used

This question deserves a direct answer. If you've been in business for more than a few years, you have almost certainly encountered EOS, Scaling Up, McKinsey 7S, or some variant of a business coaching methodology. Each of these has genuine value. Each also has a specific architectural gap that Pattern Science addresses.

EOS / Traction

EOS (the Entrepreneurial Operating System) has achieved remarkable market penetration in the founder-led business segment for a legitimate reason: it provides an accessible, structured operating system with clear components that give operationally chaotic businesses a practical framework for execution discipline. Its simplicity is its greatest commercial asset.

The architectural gap: EOS assumes that all six components should be addressed simultaneously and with equal priority. There is no constraint hierarchy, no suppression logic, no sequencing doctrine. EOS implementations that succeed typically do so in businesses that already have adequate Ownership and Clarity architecture. Implementations that fail or regress almost invariably do so because execution components are installed on top of unresolved Ownership or Clarity deficits. The structures are built; the behaviours don't lock in; regression follows.

Scaling Up / Rockefeller Habits

Scaling Up (Verne Harnish) is strong in the Clarity-to-Rhythm domain — it provides robust tools for strategy articulation, execution cadence, and people management. Its four-domain framework addresses a broader organisational scope than EOS.

The architectural gap: Scaling Up shares EOS's parallel implementation assumption. Its heavy emphasis on Execution components before establishing Ownership clarity is a sequencing vulnerability in the Founder Bottleneck archetype — the most common constraint pattern in the business segment both methodologies target.

The Coaching Industry

Business coaching's core contribution is the Behavioural Reinforcement dimension — helping leaders develop the self-awareness, communication skills, and behavioural habits that strengthen organisational culture and leadership effectiveness. When delivered into organisations with adequate structural foundations, coaching produces genuine and durable leadership development.

The architectural gap: behavioural intervention in the absence of structural architecture is the precise error that the Interpretation Doctrine™ prohibits as its first principle. When a business has an Ownership structural deficit, coaching the founder on leadership style or mindset produces temporary behavioural improvement against a structural void. The coached behaviours have no structural anchor. Within ninety days, regression is the rule, not the exception.

Pattern Science does not replace these frameworks. It provides the diagnostic and sequencing architecture that tells you which framework to apply, to which pattern, in which order. EOS Rhythm components are genuinely valuable — in a business with established Ownership and Clarity. Coaching is genuinely valuable — in a business with established structural foundations. Pattern Science is the diagnostic layer that determines when each is appropriate.

Chapter Summary

- Pattern Science is a new management discipline built on the intersection of General Systems Theory, Theory of Constraints, and Behavioural Psychology.
- It is the first discipline to treat the sequence of pattern correction as a structural necessity rather than a practitioner preference.
- Each existing framework — EOS, Scaling Up, the coaching industry — has genuine value and a specific architectural gap. Pattern Science provides the diagnostic and sequencing architecture that determines when each is appropriate.
- The central claim: durable business transformation requires identifying the primary structural constraint and correcting it first, before any downstream pattern work begins.

Chapter 5

The Ownership Pattern

From founder-driven to leader-led

Of all the patterns in the Business Alchemy™ architecture, Ownership is the one that founders most resist confronting — because confronting it means acknowledging that the business's greatest constraint is not the market, not the team, not the systems. It is the founder.

Not because founders are incapable. Quite the opposite. The Ownership pattern deficit is almost always a consequence of exceptional founder capability. The founder is genuinely the most competent person in the room. The founder does make better decisions than most of the team. The founder's involvement does produce better outcomes, in the short term.

But a business that depends on founder involvement for the quality of its decisions, the consistency of its standards, and the resolution of its problems is structurally constrained. It cannot scale beyond what the founder can personally manage. It carries key-person risk that suppresses its enterprise value. And it traps the founder in a role that generates diminishing returns on their capability over time.

The Ownership pattern is the first in the canonical sequence because its weakness suppresses everything that follows. Clarity cannot be structurally embedded when accountability is centralised at the founder. Rhythm cannot be built when leadership authority is not genuinely distributed. Flow cannot be sustained when the team's operational confidence is contingent on founder presence. Value cannot be maximised when the founder is spending their best hours on decisions that should be made at the leadership level.

What the Ownership Pattern Governs

The Ownership pattern governs the structural distribution of accountability, decision authority, and leadership responsibility across the organisation. A healthy Ownership pattern means that leaders at every level genuinely own their domain — not performatively, not when the founder is watching, but structurally: through scorecard architecture, decision ladders, and accountability rhythms that make ownership the default operating condition rather than the exception.

A compromised Ownership pattern means that real authority — the authority that is exercised when decisions are difficult, when standards are ambiguous, when conflict requires resolution — remains with the founder regardless of what the org chart says.

Science Foundation

Principal-Agent Theory (Jensen and Meckling, 1976) describes the structural challenge of delegating authority within organisations. The agent (the leader) will act in the principal's (the founder's) interest only when the structural conditions — incentives, information, and accountability mechanisms — make that alignment the path of least resistance. Self-Determination Theory (Deci and Ryan, 1985) establishes that genuine ownership requires Autonomy — the sense of genuine control over one's domain. Without structural accountability architecture, neither condition is met.

The Diagnostic Signals

Ownership pattern dysfunction presents with remarkable consistency across industries and business sizes. The language the founder uses to describe the problem will vary; the structural signature is almost always the same.

- Decisions consistently escalate to the founder regardless of who nominally owns them
- Leaders manage upward rather than managing their domain — they bring problems to the founder rather than solving them
- "I end up doing it myself in the end" — the founder's most common description of their own leadership experience
- Meeting culture is characterised by status reporting to the founder rather than leadership team problem-solving
- Accountability conversations are avoided or handled by the founder when they should be handled by the relevant leader
- New leaders quickly learn that the founder's involvement in decisions produces better short-term outcomes, and defer accordingly

! Practitioner Warning

The most dangerous Ownership pattern symptom is one that appears healthy: a high-performing leadership team that nonetheless cannot function independently. This is almost always compensating behaviour — the team performs well precisely because the founder is closely involved. Remove the founder and performance deteriorates rapidly. This is not leadership strength. It is Ownership structural fragility.

The Five Playbook Actions

Ownership pattern correction follows a specific sequence. Each action builds the structural foundation for the next. Attempting actions out of sequence — particularly deploying identity or mindset work before structural accountability architecture is established — is a sequencing error that produces temporary behaviour change without structural anchor.

Action One: The Leader Scorecard

The Leader Scorecard is the foundational accountability architecture of the Ownership pattern. It is a single-page document for each key leader that defines their five core outcome accountabilities, their ninety-day commitments against each accountability, and their self-assessment rhythm.

The Scorecard is not a job description. It is an ownership document. The difference is critical: a job description defines what a leader is responsible for doing. A Scorecard defines what outcomes a leader owns — and how they will measure their own performance against those outcomes week by week.

Scorecards must be co-created with the leader, not assigned by the founder. Co-creation is itself a structural ownership act — it builds the leader's sense of genuine authority over the domain, which Self-Determination Theory identifies as the prerequisite for intrinsic motivation and sustained ownership.

Action Two: The Decision Ladder

The Decision Ladder is a three-tier decision authority map that makes explicit what each leader can decide independently, what requires peer consultation, and what escalates to the founder or board. Its purpose is not to restrict decision-making — it is to make the implicit explicit, which is the structural prerequisite for leaders to make decisions confidently.

Most founders discover that the overwhelming majority of decisions currently escalating to them sit comfortably within the first tier of the

Decision Ladder: decisions that leaders should be making independently based on their Scorecard ownership. The escalations are happening not because the decisions require founder authority, but because the structural permission for leaders to make them has never been formally established.

The Decision Ladder formalises that permission. It does not change the capability of the leadership team. It changes the structural environment in which they operate — and as Lewin's Field Theory predicts, that environmental change produces the behavioural change that leadership development programs have been trying to produce through coaching alone.

Action Three: The Weekly Leadership Cadence

The Weekly Leadership Cadence is the rhythmic accountability structure that gives Scorecards and Decision Ladders operational reality. Without a consistent weekly meeting structure — one where leaders report on their Scorecard accountabilities, not on operational updates — the accountability architecture exists on paper but not in practice.

The cadence has a specific structure: forty-five minutes maximum, structured agenda, each leader provides a Scorecard update and flags decisions they have made or are making. The founder observes more than they direct. They ask questions; they do not solve problems. This is the most difficult behavioural shift in the Ownership correction process, and it requires structural support — which is why the Scorecard and Decision Ladder must be established first.

Action Four: The Owner-to-Founder Liberation Plan

The Liberation Plan is a structured transfer of specific decision authorities from the founder to named leaders over a ninety-day period. It is not a general aspiration to "delegate more." It is a document specifying exactly which decisions currently made by the founder will be transferred, to whom, by which date, and what support the receiving leader requires to hold the accountability.

The Liberation Plan is as much about the founder's identity as it is about operational structure. Founders who have built their identity around being the decision-maker in the room experience genuine discomfort when that role is structurally transferred. This is real, it is valid, and it is the reason why structural architecture must accompany the psychological transition rather than follow it.

Action Five: Behaviour Map™ Integration

The Behaviour Map™ — the NeuroTalent Method™ tool that maps individual behavioural styles against the five Alchemy Patterns — is deployed during Ownership correction to identify the specific behavioural demands that each leader's Ownership role places on their natural style.

A stability-style leader in a high-accountability role requires different structural support than a drive-style leader in the same role. A Precision-style founder who has been the quality authority needs different transition support than an Impact-style founder who has been the cultural authority. The Behaviour Map™ makes these distinctions explicit and translates them into specific structural and developmental recommendations.

The NeuroTalent Lens — Renae Fazakerley

The Ownership pattern is where the NeuroTalent Method™ has its highest leverage. Accountability architecture without behavioural architecture is a structural plan that doesn't account for the humans who have to operate inside it. Understanding whether a leader's natural behavioural style supports or resists ownership is the difference between a Scorecard that holds and one that's quietly ignored within six weeks.

Chapter Summary

- The Ownership pattern is Position 1 in the canonical sequence because its weakness suppresses every downstream pattern simultaneously.
- Ownership dysfunction almost always traces to exceptional founder capability creating structural centralisation, not to inadequate leadership in the team.
- The five Ownership playbook actions — Leader Scorecard, Decision Ladder, Weekly Leadership Cadence, Liberation Plan, and Behaviour Map™ Integration — must be deployed in sequence. Behavioural work before structural architecture is a sequencing error.
- The Liberation Plan is as much an identity transition for the founder as it is an operational transfer.

Chapter 6

The Clarity Pattern

From scattered activity to unified direction

If Ownership is about who leads, Clarity is about where. It is the pattern that answers the question every person in the organisation is silently asking: what are we actually trying to achieve, and how does what I do today contribute to it?

Most businesses have a version of strategic clarity. They have a vision statement, or a mission, or a three-year plan documented on a slide somewhere. What they don't have is Clarity in the structural sense that Pattern Science defines it — direction that is specific enough to filter decisions, documented enough to survive the founder's absence from a conversation, and operationalised enough that it is reflected in what gets funded, resourced, and celebrated.

The gap between having a vision and having structural Clarity is where the second most common constraint pattern in founder-led businesses lives. And it is the gap that the Strategic Chaos archetype makes so costly — because when Clarity is absent or misaligned, the Rhythm pattern directly below it in the hierarchy cannot function. Execution cadence cannot organise around a signal that keeps changing.

"Clarity only exists when it is shared, documented, and understood by the people who are executing it. Strategy

held in the founder's head is not Clarity. It is a single point of failure with very expensive consequences."

The Cross-Construct Diagnostic Trap

The Clarity pattern produces the most common cross-construct diagnostic trap in Pattern Science: High Behavioural Reinforcement paired with Low Structural Coherence.

This means the team is working genuinely hard to align with a strategic direction that isn't structurally documented or consistently communicated. Individual leaders are demonstrating high behavioural commitment to their interpretation of the strategy — but because their interpretations differ, their behaviours diverge. The business experiences this as a culture problem, a communication problem, or an alignment problem. It is a structural documentation problem.

Running a culture or communication program in this state will produce temporary improvement and rapid regression — the team's willingness to align is not the problem. The absence of something concrete to align with is the problem.

The Five Playbook Actions

Action One: The Three-Year North Star and Twelve-Month Plan

The North Star is a strategic direction document specific enough that any leader in the business could use it to filter a decision. Not a values poster. Not an aspirational statement. A document that answers three questions with operational specificity: Where is the business in three years? What must be true at twelve months for the three-year direction to be on track? What does success look and feel like at both timeframes?

The facilitation of this document is itself a structural act. When the leadership team builds the North Star together, alignment is generated through the process of construction, not through the distribution of a finished document. Leaders who help create the direction own it in a way that leaders who receive it cannot.

Action Two: The Critical Few Priorities Framework

The Critical Few is a ruthless reduction exercise. Every business generates more priorities than it can execute with quality. The Critical Few Framework identifies the three — maximum five — strategic priorities for the current ninety-day period that will most directly advance the twelve-month plan. Everything else is either delegated, deferred, or explicitly declined.

The difficulty of the Critical Few is not identifying the priorities. It is the discipline of committing to not doing the ones that don't make the list. Most founder-led businesses experience priority inflation — the gradual expansion of the "priority" list until everything is a priority and therefore nothing is. The Critical Few Framework reverses this by requiring explicit trade-offs rather than implicit accumulation.

Science Foundation

Sweller's Cognitive Load Theory (1988) establishes that when the number of competing priorities exceeds working memory capacity, decision quality degrades and execution becomes reactive rather than strategic. Miller's Law (1956) identified 7±2 meaningful chunks as the limit of working memory. A business with seventeen simultaneous priorities is not ambitious — it is cognitively overloaded.

Action Three: The Opportunity Filter

The Opportunity Filter is a decision tool that operationalises Clarity at the point where strategic discipline is most commonly lost: the moment a new opportunity appears. Most founder-led businesses have a structural weakness at this exact moment — the founder's natural optimism and opportunity-seeking behaviour creates a tendency to say yes to things that don't fit the strategy, at the cost of the execution capacity required for the things that do.

The Opportunity Filter is three to five criteria — specific to the business's current strategic direction — that every new opportunity must pass before it receives leadership attention. It is not a rigid rule; it is a structural friction mechanism that ensures opportunities are assessed against the strategy rather than against the founder's enthusiasm.

Action Four: Role Clarity Documents

Each key leader receives a single-page document defining their role's strategic contribution to the North Star, their top five outcome accountabilities, and how their role connects to the Critical Few priorities for the current quarter.

Role Clarity Documents are the bridge between organisational strategy and individual Ownership — they translate the Clarity pattern into the structural information each leader needs to exercise genuine Ownership of their domain. Without them, Ownership Scorecards float without strategic context, and leaders default to operational activity rather than strategic contribution.

Action Five: The Strategic Message Cascade

The Cascade is the process of communicating the strategic direction from the founder through the leadership team and into the organisation —

with a specific quality control mechanism: testing comprehension at each level, not just delivery.

Most strategic communications cascade by delivery: the founder presents the strategy to the leadership team, who present it to their teams. The message degrades at each level because interpretation is not tested. The Cascade addresses this by requiring each leader to present their understanding of the strategy back to the founder before communicating it to their team — a process that surfaces misalignments at the leadership level before they propagate into the organisation.

Chapter Summary

- The Clarity pattern governs strategic direction, priority architecture, and the operational translation of strategy into decisions.
- The most common Clarity diagnostic trap: High BR + Low SC. The team is working hard to align with a strategy that isn't structurally documented.
- The five Clarity playbook actions — North Star, Critical Few, Opportunity Filter, Role Clarity, and Strategic Cascade — build Clarity from strategic architecture down to individual role contribution.
- Clarity can only be addressed after Ownership is structurally established. Strategy held in the founder's head is not Clarity — it is an Ownership deficit wearing Clarity's clothes.

Chapter 7

The Rhythm Pattern

From chaos to predictable, compounding execution

Rhythm is the pattern that most businesses think they are addressing when they implement operational improvements — and the pattern that most operational improvements fail to establish.

Operational improvements — new project management tools, restructured meeting rhythms, redesigned KPI dashboards — address the infrastructure of execution. Rhythm, in the Pattern Science sense, is something deeper: the self-sustaining cadence of execution that produces consistent, predictable output regardless of who is present, what pressures are operating, or what disruptions the week introduces.

The difference between a business with established Rhythm and one with good operational infrastructure is the difference between a business that performs consistently and one that performs well when conditions are ideal. Ideal conditions are the exception. Rhythm is what sustains performance when conditions are not ideal — which is most of the time.

The Sequencing Dependency

Rhythm is Position 3 in the canonical sequence, and its dependency on both Ownership and Clarity is not theoretical — it is structural and observable.

Without Ownership: accountability rhythms — the weekly cadences, the scorecard reviews, the daily standups — require leaders who genuinely own their domain to make them real. A daily standup in a business where no one owns their commitments is a status-reporting exercise that produces minutes but not momentum.

Without Clarity: execution cadence cannot organise around a direction that keeps changing. You cannot build a predictable operating rhythm around an unpredictable strategic signal. This is the Strategic Chaos archetype's mechanism of suppression: not that the execution systems are wrong, but that they are being asked to organise around something that refuses to stay still.

⚠ Practitioner Warning

The most common Rhythm sequencing error: installing meeting structures and KPI dashboards before Ownership and Clarity are established. The structures exist. The behaviours don't lock in. The meetings drift. The dashboards stop being updated. The leader concludes that their team "won't do the system." The system was installed on an inadequate structural foundation.

The Five Playbook Actions

Action One: The Daily Huddle and Weekly Leadership Meeting

Two meeting structures form the rhythmic backbone of execution. The Daily Huddle is ten to fifteen minutes, standing, with three questions: what did I complete yesterday, what am I completing today, what is blocking me. Its purpose is not information sharing — it is the daily public commitment mechanism that sustains execution accountability without requiring management overhead.

The Weekly Leadership Meeting is forty-five minutes with a structured agenda: Scorecard review, KPI review, one strategic issue worked through to decision. The founder chairs; the leaders report. The critical discipline is that this meeting happens at the same time every week, regardless of operational pressure. When it is cancelled for operational urgency, the Rhythm pattern begins to degrade.

Action Two: Lead vs. Lag KPI Dashboard

Most businesses track only lagging indicators: revenue, margin, job completion rate, customer satisfaction. Lagging indicators tell you what happened. They cannot be acted upon in the current period because they describe the past.

Leading indicators tell you what is going to happen. They are the activities that, when performed at the right volume and quality, reliably produce the lagging outcomes. Sales conversations lead revenue. Site inspections lead quality scores. Training hours lead capability metrics.

A Lead-Lag dashboard creates Rhythm by giving leaders indicators they can act on in real time, rather than indicators they can only observe with regret. When the leading indicators are green, the lagging indicators will follow. When leading indicators deteriorate, the lagging outcomes can be prevented rather than reported.

Action Three: Quarterly Strategic Review and Reset

The quarterly rhythm is the strategic heartbeat of the Rhythm pattern — the cadence at which the business steps back from execution to review progress against the twelve-month plan, reset the Critical Few priorities, surface new constraints, and celebrate the momentum that has been generated.

The Quarterly Review is not an operational meeting. It is a strategic governance event with a defined agenda: PDI comparative review, twelve-month plan progress assessment, Critical Few retrospective, Critical Few reset for next quarter. It reinforces the Clarity pattern from above and gives the daily and weekly rhythms their strategic context.

Action Four: Project Rhythm Maps

For businesses with project-based delivery, the Project Rhythm Map converts individual project execution from improvised responses to customer timelines into a replicable cadence: what happens in Week 1 of every project, Week 2, Week 3. The rhythm of the project type becomes an organisational standard rather than a project manager's personal approach.

Project Rhythm Maps produce two structural outcomes: they make delivery predictable for clients and they make capacity planning possible for the business. Without them, project managers operate as individual execution islands, and the business's delivery consistency is entirely dependent on the quality of the individual managing each project.

Action Five: Operational Capacity Planning

Rhythm breaks when capacity is chronically exceeded. No meeting structure or KPI framework can sustain execution discipline in a business that is consistently asking its people to do more than they can do well.

Operational Capacity Planning is a simple model that makes the business's capacity constraint visible: how much work can the team absorb per week or month, what is current utilisation, where are the bottlenecks, and what is the decision framework for managing above-capacity periods. It converts an invisible constraint into a managed operational variable.

Chapter Summary

- Rhythm is the self-sustaining execution cadence that produces consistent, predictable output regardless of conditions. It is not the same as operational infrastructure.
- Rhythm is suppressed by both Ownership deficits and Clarity misalignment. Sequencing error — installing Rhythm before Ownership and Clarity are established — is the most common cause of meeting structures that drift and KPIs that stop being updated.
- The five Rhythm playbook actions — Daily Huddle, Weekly Meeting, Lead-Lag Dashboard, Quarterly Review, and Capacity Planning — build from operational cadence to strategic governance.

Chapter 8

The Flow Pattern

From friction to collaborative momentum

The Flow pattern is the most emotionally compelling pattern in the Business Alchemy™ architecture — and the most commonly misdiagnosed one.

When Flow is disrupted — when there is tension between departments, communication breakdown between leaders, cultural friction or burnout in the team — these symptoms are highly visible, emotionally felt, and narratively compelling. Founders and leadership teams experience them acutely. And because the symptoms are so visible, they appear to be the primary problem.

The Interpretation Doctrine™ is explicit: Flow problems are almost always downstream of structural failures in Ownership, Clarity, or Rhythm. The communication breakdown is happening because the execution environment is chaotic and unpredictable — a Rhythm failure. The cultural friction is happening because no one agrees on where the business is going — a Clarity failure. The burnout is happening because leaders are compensating for an accountability structure that doesn't exist — an Ownership failure.

This does not mean Flow problems are not real. They are real and they matter. It means that direct Flow intervention before upstream structural correction is a sequencing error that will produce temporary improvement and rapid regression.

The NeuroTalent Method™ and the Flow Pattern

The Flow pattern is where Renae Fazakerley's NeuroTalent Method™ has its deepest contribution to the Business Alchemy™ architecture.

Structural diagnosis can identify that a Flow pattern deficit exists. It can identify that leadership cohesion is low, that communication is breaking down, that cultural friction is suppressing collaborative performance. What structural diagnosis cannot do — what no pattern-level diagnostic can do — is explain the specific human dynamics that are generating the friction, and prescribe the specific behavioural and communication interventions that will address them.

The NeuroTalent Method™ fills that gap. It maps the behavioural architecture of individuals and teams — understanding not just how people behave but why they behave that way, what drives them, what depletes them, and what communication environment they need to perform at their highest level. Applied within the Flow pattern, it transforms interpersonal friction from an emotionally charged mystery into a structurally legible and therefore solvable problem.

The NeuroTalent Lens — Renae Fazakerley

The NeuroTalent Method™ was built on a foundational insight: that most recruitment and leadership development fails not because it misidentifies capability, but because it misunderstands motivation. You can hire the right skills into the wrong behavioural environment and produce exactly the friction and underperformance you were trying to avoid. The NeuroTalent lens doesn't just help you understand your current team's dynamics — it changes how you build teams from the start.

The Five Playbook Actions

Action One: Behaviour Map for the Leadership Team

Administering the Behaviour Map for all key leaders is the first Flow correction action — and it produces the most immediate and practically useful output of any diagnostic in the Business Alchemy™ suite. The Behaviour Map™ maps each leader's natural style across the four dimensions and connects that profile directly to the demands of their Ownership pattern role.

The output is not a personality label. It is a structural insight: this leader's natural style creates predictable friction at these specific points in the business's operating cadence, and these structural and communication adjustments will reduce that friction without requiring the leader to become a different person.

Action Two: The Rules of Engagement Framework

The Rules of Engagement is a co-created set of team operating agreements — not a values poster, not a cultural aspiration document, but a specific behavioural operating system: how we communicate difficult information, how we make decisions together, how we handle disagreement, how we give feedback, how we hold each other to commitments. Made explicit before a conflict occurs rather than during one.

The distinction between Rules of Engagement and cultural values is important and frequently confused. Values describe what the organisation believes. Rules of Engagement describe how the organisation operates. Both matter; neither substitutes for the other.

Action Three: Communication Mapping

Using the Behaviour Map™ outputs, the Communication Map translates individual profiles into practical guidance: how each leader prefers to receive information (written or verbal, structured or exploratory), how they prefer to receive feedback (direct or contextualised, frequent or periodic), what communication environment brings out their best performance, and what communication approaches activate their stress responses.

The Communication Map is shared with all leaders — it makes the invisible legible and converts interpersonal friction from a personality conflict into a communication mismatch that has a structural solution.

Action Four: The Conflict Resolution Operating System

A structured conflict resolution approach — agreed before conflict occurs — is one of the highest-leverage structural investments available to a leadership team. When conflict arises without a defined resolution process, it defaults to the most hierarchically powerful person's preferred approach, which is almost always the founder's approach and almost always reinforces rather than resolves the underlying tension.

The Conflict Resolution Operating System defines: when issues are addressed directly between leaders, when a third party is involved, what constitutes an escalation to the founder, and what behaviours are outside the range of acceptable conduct in any conflict context. Its value is not primarily in the process — it is in the psychological safety it creates by making the process predictable before the conflict makes everything unpredictable.

Action Five: Energy Mapping at the Leadership Level

The final Flow action is the most nuanced: mapping where each leader's energy is highest and lowest relative to their current role, and identifying the role-style misalignments that are creating chronic Flow suppression regardless of structural improvements.

A high-Precision leader in a high-Drive role will create quality bottlenecks that suppress delivery Rhythm regardless of how sound the Rhythm structures are. A high-Stability leader in a high-accountability Ownership role will avoid the difficult conversations that accountability requires regardless of how clear the Scorecard is. Energy mapping makes these misalignments visible — not to judge them, but to accommodate them structurally.

Chapter Summary

- The Flow pattern is the most commonly misdiagnosed primary constraint in founder-led businesses. Its symptoms are highly visible and emotionally compelling; its causes are almost always upstream structural failures.
- The NeuroTalent Method™ provides the human behavioural architecture that structural pattern diagnosis alone cannot supply — translating interpersonal friction from an emotional mystery into a structurally legible and solvable problem.
- The five Flow playbook actions — Behaviour Map™, Rules of Engagement, Communication Mapping, Conflict Resolution System, and Energy Mapping — build from individual profiling to team operating system.
- Flow intervention before Rhythm is established will produce temporary cohesion and rapid regression. The team needs a predictable operational environment before relational cohesion is possible.

Chapter 9

The Value Pattern

From activity to high-leverage commercial architecture

The Value pattern is where the upstream work of Pattern Science produces its most commercially visible outcomes. By the time a business reaches Value in the canonical sequence with healthy Ownership, Clarity, Rhythm, and Flow in place, the commercial leverage available is significantly greater than anything achievable through direct Value intervention alone.

This is the Momentum-to-Valuation chain that Pattern Science documents: Pattern Alignment produces Structural Coherence. Structural Coherence produces Outcome Predictability. Outcome Predictability reduces Risk. Risk Reduction improves EBITDA Quality. EBITDA Quality drives Valuation Multiple. Valuation Multiple creates Enterprise Value.

Every step in this chain is a consequence of the step before it. Enterprise value is not created by a pricing strategy or a margin improvement program. It is created by structural pattern alignment that produces the outcome predictability and reduced risk that buyers and investors price as a premium.

The Fragility Signal

The most consequential Value pattern diagnostic finding is not low EBITDA. It is high EBITDA without upstream structural integrity.

A business with strong commercial performance but compromised Ownership, Clarity, Rhythm, or Flow is structurally fragile under scale conditions. It is performing well in the current conditions. The foundation will not support growth, succession, or investor scrutiny. Buyers and investors price this fragility. Founders who attempt to sell or raise capital from this structural position almost always encounter a valuation that feels punitive but is actually precise — the market is pricing the structural risk that the founder has adapted around too completely to see.

The Five Playbook Actions

Action One: The Margin Diagnostic Review

The Margin Diagnostic is a bottom-up profitability analysis by revenue stream, client, project type, or service line. Its purpose is to make the Pareto distribution of your commercial performance visible: the twenty percent of activities that generate eighty percent of your profit, and the activities consuming disproportionate capacity for insufficient return.

Most businesses have a sense of their profitable and unprofitable activities. The Margin Diagnostic makes it structural — producing a evidence base that the leadership team can use to make resource allocation decisions rather than relying on founder intuition.

Action Two: The Value Ladder

The Value Ladder maps all current revenue lines by their effort-to-margin ratio and plots a strategic direction for the revenue mix: which activities should be scaled, which maintained, which exited. It translates the Margin Diagnostic from an analysis into a commercial strategy.

The Value Ladder conversation is frequently one of the most confronting exercises in the Business Alchemy™ engagement — because it often reveals that the business's largest revenue source is not its most profitable one, and that growth in the wrong direction has been consuming capacity that should have been directed elsewhere.

Action Three: The Pricing Strategy Reset

Pricing in founder-led businesses is almost always systematically low. Not because the founder doesn't understand value — but because pricing decisions are made intuitively rather than structurally, and the structural tendency is to anchor to cost-plus rather than to value-based pricing logic.

The Pricing Strategy Reset is a structured process — not a sudden price increase — that builds the commercial case for value-based pricing, designs a ninety-day client migration plan, and establishes pricing architecture that can be sustained and defended without founder involvement in individual pricing decisions.

Action Four: The Customer Quality Framework

The Customer Quality Framework is a client filter — three to five criteria that define an ideal client versus a margin-draining client, applied to the existing client base and to all future client acquisition. It is the commercial expression of the Opportunity Filter from the Clarity pattern: a structural mechanism that prevents the business from saying yes to work that consumes capacity without commensurate return.

The Customer Quality Framework also provides the foundation for a client exit strategy — the structured process of disengaging from bottom-tier clients in a way that preserves relationship quality while freeing capacity for higher-return work.

Action Five: The Quarterly Value Review

The Quarterly Value Review establishes commercial performance as a standing leadership conversation rather than a finance function report. It is a sixty-minute quarterly session with the leadership team reviewing margin by stream, Value Ladder progress, pricing architecture, and the client portfolio — against the metrics established in the Margin Diagnostic and the targets set in the Value Ladder.

The Quarterly Value Review reinforces the connection between the leadership team's Ownership and Clarity work and the commercial outcomes that work is meant to generate — closing the loop between structural pattern alignment and enterprise value creation.

Chapter Summary

- The Value pattern is where the upstream work of Pattern Science produces its most commercially visible outcomes. Each upstream pattern alignment creates leverage that compounds at the Value level.
- High EBITDA without upstream structural integrity is a fragility signal, not a success signal. Buyers and investors price this structural risk precisely.
- The Momentum-to-Valuation chain connects pattern alignment directly to enterprise value: Pattern Alignment to Structural Coherence to Outcome Predictability to Risk Reduction to EBITDA Quality to Valuation Multiple to Enterprise Value.
- The five Value playbook actions — Margin Diagnostic, Value Ladder, Pricing Reset, Customer Quality Framework, and

Quarterly Value Review — build commercial architecture from evidence to strategy to governance.

Part Three
The Practice

"Diagnosis without action is just therapy."

— Pattern Science™

Chapter 10

How to Read Your Business

A self-diagnostic guide before you run the PDI

Before you administer the Pattern Disruption Index™, there is a diagnostic act you can perform right now, with nothing but this book and your honest attention to the business you run every day.

It won't give you the precision of the PDI. It won't produce a suppression map or a constraint hierarchy. But it will do something the PDI cannot do on its own: it will activate your pattern awareness — the capacity to see your business structurally rather than symptomatically. And that capacity is the most practically valuable thing this book can give you.

Work through the following questions honestly. Don't answer based on how you want the business to be. Answer based on what you observe when you're not in the room — or more precisely, what happens in the business when you are in the room and what stops happening when you're not.

Reading the Ownership Pattern

The Ownership pattern is the easiest to misread because its dysfunction so closely resembles strength. A founder who is deeply involved in every decision, who maintains high standards across every domain, who is genuinely the most capable person in most rooms — looks like an asset.

The Ownership pattern deficit is precisely that asset becoming a structural constraint.

Ask yourself the following:

- When you are absent from a meeting, do decisions get made or deferred?
- In the last month, how many decisions landed on your desk that should have been made by someone else? What stopped that person from making them?
- If you left the business for four weeks, which parts would continue to function and which would revert to you remotely?
- When a leader in your business makes a decision you disagree with, what happens? Do they hold their position or do they defer to yours?
- Can each of your key leaders articulate, in specific terms, what outcomes they personally own — not what they are responsible for doing, but what results they are accountable for producing?

If your honest answers reveal that decisions flow toward you, that your absence creates stasis, that your leaders manage upward rather than managing their domain — your Ownership pattern is compromised. The question is whether it is absent (never built), misaligned (built incorrectly), or suppressed (built correctly but not functioning because something upstream isn't working— though in Ownership's case, there is no upstream pattern, so suppression is impossible: if Ownership is low, it is absent or misaligned).

The Pattern Insight

> *The most common misreading of the Ownership pattern: the founder concludes their leaders lack capability because they won't make decisions independently. In the vast majority of cases, the leaders are capable. The structural permission to decide has never been formally established. Capability and permission are not the same thing.*

Reading the Clarity Pattern

The Clarity pattern is the one most founders believe they have. They have a vision. They have communicated it. They have a strategy document somewhere. The diagnostic question is not whether Clarity exists in the founder's mind — it is whether Clarity is structurally embedded in the organisation's daily decision-making.

- Ask three leaders in your business, separately, to describe the company's top three priorities for the next ninety days. Compare the answers. Do they match?
- In the last quarter, how many new opportunities, projects, or initiatives did the business take on? How many of them were assessed against a formal strategic filter before receiving leadership attention?
- Can any leader in the business, without reference to any document, describe where the business will be in three years and what must be true at twelve months for that direction to be on track?
- When a decision needs to be made about resource allocation — which project gets the best team, which client gets prioritised, which initiative gets funded — what is the decision framework? Is it explicit and structural, or is it the founder's instinct applied case by case?

- How many times in the last month has a new "priority" been added to the business's existing list of priorities without something else being explicitly removed?

Divergent answers to the first question are the clearest possible signal of a Clarity deficit. When different leaders describe different priorities, it is not a communication problem. It is a structural documentation problem. The strategy exists in the founder's head and has been interpreted differently by every leader who has been exposed to fragments of it.

Reading the Rhythm Pattern

Rhythm is the pattern that reveals itself most clearly in the texture of the working week. You don't need a diagnostic instrument to feel a Rhythm deficit — you feel it every Sunday evening when you anticipate the week ahead.

- Does the business have a fixed weekly leadership meeting that happens at the same time every week regardless of operational pressure? When was the last time it was cancelled?
- Do the leaders in your business know, on a Monday morning, their three most important commitments for the week — and do they review those commitments the following Monday?
- What are the leading indicators in your business? Not the lagging results — the activities that, when performed at the right volume and quality, reliably produce the outcomes you want. Can every leader name them?
- When a project or client engagement goes off track, how quickly does the business know? Is the signal a lagging financial result or a leading operational indicator?

- Does the business have a quarterly strategic review — a formal moment where the leadership team steps back from execution to assess progress and reset priorities?

A business with established Rhythm feels different from the inside. There is a predictable operational heartbeat. People know what they are doing this week because last week's review made it clear and this week's commitments were publicly declared. The absence of that heartbeat is Rhythm dysfunction — and it almost always traces to an upstream Ownership or Clarity problem that is preventing the rhythm from being meaningful.

Reading the Flow Pattern

Flow is the pattern where the diagnostic instinct most commonly goes wrong. Its symptoms — interpersonal friction, communication breakdown, cultural deterioration, burnout — are emotionally compelling and narratively powerful. They feel like primary problems. In Pattern Science, they are almost always secondary symptoms of upstream structural failures.

The diagnostic discipline with Flow is to read it twice: once to understand the symptom, and once to identify the upstream pattern that is generating it.

- When there is tension between individuals or departments in your business, what is the structural explanation? Not the interpersonal one — the structural one. What ambiguity, what absent process, what competing priority is the friction expressing?
- Are your best performers performing because the structure supports them or despite the structure? What would they tell you if they were being completely candid about what frustrates them?

- In the last three months, have any strong performers left the business or significantly reduced their engagement? What was the structural condition they were operating in?
- Does your leadership team make decisions together, or do they make decisions individually and defend their positions in leadership meetings?
- When a difficult interpersonal situation arises between two leaders, is there a defined process for resolution, or does it default to the most powerful person's preferred approach?

Practitioner Warning

If your Flow scores are low, resist the instinct to intervene directly. Before commissioning a team workshop, a culture survey, or a leadership coach, ask: what is the upstream structural condition generating this symptom? In the majority of cases, Flow problems are Rhythm, Clarity, or Ownership problems that have been misread as people problems. Fix the upstream pattern and watch what happens to the team dynamic.

Reading the Value Pattern

The Value pattern is the most commercially visible and the most structurally dependent. Its dysfunction is easy to identify — declining margins, inconsistent profitability, revenue that doesn't translate to cash — but the diagnostic error is almost always to treat the Value symptom as the Value problem.

- Do you know, right now, which twenty percent of your revenue activities generate eighty percent of your profit? Not instinctively — structurally, with data?
- When was the last time you explicitly declined work because it didn't meet a defined profitability threshold?

- Are your prices set by a value-based framework or by what you think the market will accept? When did you last formally review your pricing architecture?
- Can you forecast your EBITDA for the next quarter within ten percent accuracy? If not, what is the structural reason for that unpredictability?
- What percentage of your revenue comes from your top three clients? Is that concentration a commercial vulnerability or a deliberate strategy?

A low Value score almost always means one of two things. Either the upstream patterns — Ownership, Clarity, Rhythm, Flow — have not established the structural conditions that allow commercial discipline to be exercised consistently. Or the Value architecture itself — the pricing model, the client mix, the margin framework — has never been deliberately designed.

In the first case, direct Value intervention will produce temporary improvement and regression. Fix the upstream patterns. In the second case, the Value playbook actions — Margin Diagnostic, Value Ladder, Pricing Reset, Customer Quality Framework — will produce durable improvement because the structural foundation is sound.

Putting It Together – Your Initial Pattern Reading

Having worked through the questions above, you now have an informal reading of your five patterns. It is not precise — that is what the PDI is for. But it should have surfaced at least one pattern that feels more structurally compromised than the others, and at least one pattern where the symptoms you have been addressing directly are almost certainly downstream of an upstream constraint you haven't corrected.

The most important thing the self-diagnostic gives you is not a score. It is a frame. Once you can see your business as a pattern system rather than a collection of problems, the nature of the work changes. You stop asking "what is wrong?" and start asking "what is generating this?" That question — consistently applied — is the beginning of Pattern Science in practice.

The Pattern Insight

If you have completed this self-diagnostic honestly and one pattern is clearly lower than the others, do not start there. Identify whether it is the primary constraint or a suppressed symptom. The lowest score is almost never the primary constraint. Ask: what upstream pattern, if it were corrected, would most directly improve the performance of the pattern I'm reading as low?

The Pattern Disruption Index™ makes this precise. It produces the suppression map, the constraint hierarchy, and the intervention sequence that this self-diagnostic can gesture toward but cannot fully determine. If you are ready to move from informal reading to structural diagnosis, the next chapter explains exactly how the PDI works and what it produces.

Chapter Summary

- The Ownership pattern deficit looks like strength from the inside. The diagnostic question is not whether the founder is capable but whether the structural conditions for distributed accountability exist.
- Clarity is not the founder's vision. It is the degree to which that vision is structurally documented and consistently understood by the people executing it. Test it by asking three leaders independently.
- Rhythm reveals itself in the texture of the working week. A business with established Rhythm has a predictable operational heartbeat. A business without it is permanently reactive.

- Flow problems are almost always upstream structural failures misread as people problems. Before intervening in the team dynamic, identify the structural condition generating the friction.
- The Value pattern is the output of the system. It cannot be sustainably improved by direct commercial intervention when upstream patterns are structurally deficient.
- The self-diagnostic is a frame, not a score. Its purpose is to activate structural thinking about your business before the PDI makes that thinking precise.

Chapter 11

The Pattern Disruption Index™

How to see your business structurally

Everything in Pattern Science begins with diagnosis.

Not the kind of diagnosis that produces a list of things that need to be fixed. The kind of diagnosis that produces a structural map — a picture of which patterns are generating which outcomes, which patterns are suppressing which others, and what the correct sequence of intervention is before any action is taken.

The Pattern Disruption Index™ (PDI) is the diagnostic instrument of Pattern Science. It measures your business across the five patterns and three performance constructs — Structural Coherence, Behavioural Reinforcement, and Outcome Stability — and produces a suppression map and constraint hierarchy that determines the intervention sequence.

What it does not do is tell you what's wrong. Every diagnostic tool can do that. The PDI tells you what's suppressing what — the structural intelligence that makes every subsequent intervention land in the right order.

The Three Performance Constructs

Each pattern is assessed across three constructs. Understanding these three constructs — and critically, understanding their interactions — is the diagnostic capability that separates structural diagnosis from superficial scoring.

Structural Coherence

Structural Coherence measures whether the infrastructure of the pattern exists, is correctly configured, and is aligned to organisational purpose. It answers the question: does the architecture of this pattern make sense?

A high Structural Coherence score means the formal system is sound. A low SC score means the infrastructure is absent, inconsistent, or misaligned. Structural Coherence is the most important construct for intervention sequencing, because it is the construct that upstream patterns suppress.

Behavioural Reinforcement

Behavioural Reinforcement measures whether the people in the system are consistently acting in ways that support and strengthen the pattern. A high BR score means the team's daily actions are reinforcing the pattern's structural logic. A low BR score means behaviours are working against the structural design.

The most important cross-construct interaction in the entire PDI: High BR paired with Low SC means the team is masking a structural deficit through extraordinary individual effort. The system looks functional. It is fragile. Any withdrawal of the compensating effort exposes the structural void underneath.

Outcome Stability

Outcome Stability measures whether the pattern is consistently producing reliable, predictable results. Low Outcome Stability despite adequate Structural Coherence is the primary signal of external distortion — an upstream pattern is suppressing the downstream pattern's output despite the downstream infrastructure being sound. This is the diagnostic signature of suppression, not misalignment.

The Suppression Mapping Process

Before interpreting individual pattern scores, the Interpretation Doctrine™ requires that a suppression map be completed. This is a non-negotiable pre-interpretation step that prevents the most common diagnostic error: treating a suppressed pattern as though it were the primary constraint.

The suppression mapping process works as follows:

- Review the canonical sequence: Ownership, Clarity, Rhythm, Flow, Value
- Identify which patterns score below threshold on Structural Coherence
- Map whether those structural deficits are creating downstream depression in adjacent patterns
- Mark suppressing patterns (the root cause) versus suppressed patterns (the downstream effect)
- Validate the map against the pre-engagement discovery conversation

The suppression map produced by this process is the foundational document of every Business Alchemy™ engagement. It determines the intervention sequence. No action is recommended, and no program is designed, until the suppression map is complete and validated.

The Interpretation Doctrine™

The Interpretation Doctrine™ is the formal governance document that makes Pattern Science a discipline rather than a framework. It specifies, with formal precision, how PDI data is read, how the constraint hierarchy is determined, and what intervention sequence is mandated.

Its most important principles, restated for the business owner reading this book rather than the certified practitioner:

- Structure before behaviour: do not address behavioural patterns before structural foundations are established
- Constraint before symptom: do not address the visible symptom before identifying and sequencing the structural constraint
- Suppression before direct intervention: do not apply direct correction to a suppressed pattern before correcting the upstream suppressor
- Sequence before action: do not begin any intervention without first establishing the complete constraint hierarchy

"The Doctrine is not a consulting preference. It is the formal governance of what makes intervention durable rather than temporary. Violating it produces the six-month regression that most business owners have already experienced somewhere in their advisory history."

— Interpretation Doctrine v1.0

Chapter Summary

- The PDI measures each of the five patterns across three constructs: Structural Coherence, Behavioural Reinforcement, and Outcome Stability.
- The suppression map must be completed before any individual pattern scores are interpreted. It is the structural pre-interpretation discipline that prevents the most common diagnostic error.
- The Interpretation Doctrine™ is the formal governance document specifying how diagnostic data is read and sequenced. Its four core principles: structure before behaviour, constraint before symptom, suppression before direct intervention, sequence before action.

A Worked Suppression Map – Reading a Real Business

A story from the field.

The following is a real engagement, anonymised. It illustrates how the PDI suppression map is read in practice — and why the constraint the founder identified was not the constraint the diagnostic revealed.

The Presenting Problem

A building industry business at approximately $10 million in revenue called me in with a clear diagnosis already formed: the team lacked skills. Projects were running over time and over budget. The sales team and the production team were in persistent conflict. Decisions were slow. The founder and executive team were firefighting constantly, and the business was operating in what everyone inside it described, consistently, as chaos.

The founder's view was that the solution was training and capability development. Better project managers. A more commercial sales team.

Individual performance management for the leaders who weren't performing.

Before agreeing to any of that, I ran the PDI.

The PDI Results – Before

The diagnostic came back across all five patterns and three constructs. The picture was not what the founder expected.

Ownership: Structural Coherence — LOW. Behavioural Reinforcement — LOW. Outcome Stability — LOW.

No accountability architecture existed. The founder and two senior executives were the de facto decision-making system for the entire business. Leaders below them had nominal accountability — job descriptions, KPIs on paper — but no genuine ownership of outcomes. Decisions escalated constantly. When a project manager encountered a problem, the reflex was to bring it upward. When the executive team encountered a conflict between sales and production, the reflex was to manage it personally rather than build the structural conditions that would allow both teams to resolve it themselves.

Clarity: Structural Coherence — LOW. Behavioural Reinforcement — MEDIUM. Outcome Stability — LOW.

The high behavioural reinforcement relative to low structural coherence was the first significant diagnostic signal. The team was working hard and genuinely trying to align — but there was nothing structurally documented to align with. The strategic direction existed in the founder's head. Each executive had their own interpretation of the priorities. Sales was optimising for revenue. Production was optimising for delivery quality. Neither was wrong. But they were optimising against different versions of what the business was trying to achieve, and no shared document reconciled those versions.

Rhythm: Structural Coherence — LOW. Behavioural Reinforcement — LOW. Outcome Stability — LOW.

No consistent meeting cadence. No lead-lag KPI framework. Project reviews were reactive — triggered by problems rather than scheduled as a governance rhythm. The weekly leadership meeting existed in name but drifted in format, attendance, and agenda depending on the operational pressure of the week. In high-pressure periods — which was most of the time — it was cancelled entirely.

Flow: Structural Coherence — LOW. Behavioural Reinforcement — MEDIUM. Outcome Stability — LOW.

The friction between sales and production was real and visible. But the diagnostic told a more precise story: the friction was not primarily interpersonal. It was structural. Sales were making promises to clients that production hadn't been consulted on. Production were making delivery decisions that affected client relationships without telling sales. Both teams were operating in information silos, not because they didn't want to collaborate, but because no structural mechanism — no shared KPIs, no handoff process, no regular cross-functional cadence — made collaboration the path of least resistance.

Value: Structural Coherence — LOW. Behavioural Reinforcement — LOW. Outcome Stability — LOW.

Gross margin was inconsistent and unpredictable. The leadership team didn't know which projects, which clients, or which service lines were profitable. The margin data existed in the accounting system but wasn't being translated into operational decisions. Jobs were being quoted and accepted based on revenue availability rather than margin analysis. The business was busy. It was not particularly profitable.

Reading the Suppression Map

The suppression map from this diagnostic was unambiguous. Ownership was absent — not misaligned, not suppressed, but structurally absent. No accountability architecture had ever been deliberately built. The business had grown from a small operation where the founder's direct involvement in every decision was efficient, and the structural evolution that should have accompanied that growth had never happened.

That absent Ownership pattern was suppressing everything downstream. Clarity was compromised because strategy couldn't be structurally documented and distributed without leaders who genuinely owned their domains. Rhythm was absent because execution cadence couldn't be sustained without accountability architecture to give it meaning. Flow was fractured because the inter-team friction was a symptom of absent Clarity — two teams optimising against different unstated priorities. Value was suppressed because commercial discipline requires the structural foundation of the four patterns above it.

The founder's diagnosis — a skills problem — was not what the data showed. The team was not unskilled. They were structurally unsupported. The project managers weren't making poor decisions because they lacked capability. They were avoiding decisions because the structural permission and accountability architecture for them to make decisions had never been established.

From the Field

When I presented the suppression map to the founder and executive team, the first response was resistance. The founder had been certain the problem was capability. Reframing it as a structural accountability deficit felt, initially, like an excuse for the team. It took a specific conversation — walking through each decision that had escalated to the executive team in the previous month and asking whether the person who escalated it was genuinely incapable of making it — to shift the frame. In almost every case, the answer was no. The person was capable. The structural permission to decide had never been granted.

The Intervention Sequence – First 90 Days

The primary constraint was Ownership. The intervention sequence followed the Doctrine: Ownership first, exclusively, until structural coherence was established.

Weeks 1-4: Ownership Infrastructure

Leader Scorecards were co-created with each member of the executive team. Five outcome accountabilities each. Ninety-day commitments. A self-assessment rhythm built into the weekly cadence. The process of co-creation was itself the first ownership act — for many of the leaders, it was the first time they had been asked to define what they owned rather than simply being told what to do.

A Decision Ladder was built for the business. Three tiers: decisions each leader makes independently, decisions requiring peer consultation, decisions escalating to the founder. The founder's discovery during this process was significant: approximately 80% of the decisions currently landing on his desk sat comfortably in Tier 1. They were escalating not because they required his authority but because the structural permission for leaders to decide had never been made explicit.

Weeks 5-8: Executive Function And Cadence

The Weekly Executive Meeting was restructured. Forty-five minutes, fixed agenda: Scorecard review, three KPIs per leader, one strategic issue worked through to decision. The founder chaired but did not solve. His role shifted from answering questions to asking them. This was the most difficult behavioural transition in the engagement — a founder who had built the business on the quality of his own judgement, now deliberately restraining that judgement to create space for his team's.

Decision rights were formalised. The Liberation Plan specified twelve decisions currently made by the founder that would transfer to named leaders over the ninety-day period, with dates and support structures for each transfer.

Weeks 9–12: Consolidation And Clarity Foundation

With Ownership architecture in place and beginning to stabilise — leaders using their Scorecards, the weekly meeting holding its structure, decisions being made at the right level — the Clarity work began in parallel. The North Star document was facilitated with the full executive team. For the first time, the business had a single written strategic direction that every leader had helped create and every leader could articulate.

Critically: sales and production were both in the room when the North Star was built. For the first time, both teams were working from the same strategic document rather than their own interpretations of the founder's unstated priorities. The inter-team friction reduced almost immediately — not because the relationship between the teams had been managed, but because the structural ambiguity that was generating the conflict had been removed.

The Intervention Sequence – Days 91–180

The re-PDI at Day 90 showed the first structural shift. Ownership had moved from absent to partially established — Structural Coherence rising, Behavioural Reinforcement following. The constraint hierarchy for the second 90-day cycle was clear: consolidate Ownership behavioural lock-in, build Rhythm, allow Flow to improve as a natural consequence of Clarity and Rhythm being established.

Rhythm Installation

A Lead-Lag KPI dashboard was built for the business. For a building company, the leading indicators were specific: number of jobs quoted, quote-to-win ratio by project type, percentage of active projects on programme at week three of delivery, and materials procurement lead time against project start date. These were indicators the team could act on in real time — not lagging revenue and margin figures that told them what had already happened.

Project Rhythm Maps were created for the three primary project types in the business. Each map specified what happened in each week of delivery — client communication touchpoints, internal progress reviews, cost-to-complete updates. Project delivery stopped being improvised against client timelines and became a replicable cadence. Delivery consistency improved within the first project cycle.

Flow Resolution

With Clarity documented and Rhythm establishing, the Flow pattern shifted without direct intervention — exactly as the suppression logic predicted. The sales and production conflict reduced as both teams began operating from the same strategic direction and the same operational cadence. A Rules of Engagement framework was co-created to formalise the handoff process between the two teams — not to manage the relationship, but to make the structural interface between them explicit and predictable.

The Outcome – Six Months

The PDI at Month 6 showed the business had moved from low execution risk to medium — structural coherence established across Ownership, Clarity, and Rhythm, with Flow and Value showing genuine improvement for the first time.

The commercial outcome was the one that mattered most to the founder. Gross margin improved from approximately 30% to 45% — not because the market had changed, not because the team had been replaced, but because the Value pattern now had the structural foundation to express itself. Leaders who genuinely owned their project outcomes began managing margin actively. Jobs that shouldn't have been quoted were declined. Scope creep that had previously been absorbed silently was identified, priced, and charged. The pricing decisions that had previously floated up to the founder now had structural homes at the project manager level, with a clear framework for when to escalate.

Cash flow became consistent and forecastable. Within two quarters of the Rhythm pattern being established, the leadership team could forecast EBITDA within ten percent accuracy — a capability the business had never had before. Not because the numbers had changed, but because the structural predictability that makes numbers forecastable had been built.

"The team wasn't the problem. They were operating in a structural void. Give people the architecture to own their outcomes and most of them will. The ones who don't — that's when you have a genuine capability conversation."

What the Worked Example Demonstrates

This engagement illustrates the three most important principles of Pattern Science in a single case:

- The presenting problem was wrong. The founder's diagnosis — a skills deficit — was a symptom of the Ownership pattern failure. Training the team on top of an absent Ownership structure would have produced temporary improvement and rapid regression. The people were already capable. The structure wasn't.
- The sequence was everything. Fixing Flow directly — which is what a culture or team-building intervention would have done — would have addressed the symptom while leaving the Ownership and Clarity constraints intact. The inter-team friction resolved naturally once those upstream patterns were corrected.
- The Value pattern cannot be engineered directly. The margin improvement was a consequence of structural pattern alignment, not a commercial initiative. When leaders own their outcomes, when the strategic direction is clear, when the execution cadence is predictable — commercial performance follows. It is the output of the system, not a separate intervention.

Chapter 12

The 90-Day Alchemy Cycle

Turning diagnosis into structural momentum

Diagnosis without a structured path to action is insight without leverage. The 90-Day Alchemy Cycle is the vehicle that carries Pattern Science from the diagnostic map to structural change.

Ninety days is not an arbitrary timeframe. It is long enough to establish structural coherence in a pattern — to build the infrastructure, stabilise the behaviours, and observe the early outcome signals. It is short enough to maintain urgency, force prioritisation, and sustain the leadership attention that structural transformation requires.

The 90-Day Cycle follows a three-phase structure derived from Lewin's Unfreeze-Change-Refreeze model: Diagnostic (unfreezing the current state through pattern visibility), Interpretation and Planning (designing the structural correction in sequence), and Execution (the ninety-day intervention cycle with weekly review and re-PDI at Day 90).

Phase One: The Diagnostic

The PDI is administered across the leadership team. Discovery conversations surface the pre-engagement language — the way the business describes its own constraints before the structural analysis provides a more precise frame. The suppression map is completed and validated. The constraint hierarchy is established.

This phase produces the single most important document in the engagement: the Suppression Map. It is presented to the leadership team — not as a report card, not as a scoring exercise, but as a structural picture of what is generating what.

From the Field

Two founders had built a construction business to $10 million in three years. When I presented the suppression map, the room went quiet. Then one of them leaned forward: 'Finally. We will fix this properly so we can scale.' That is the moment the engagement shifts from advisory to transformation — not when the problem is identified, but when the sequence is. They had known something was wrong. What they hadn't had was a structural explanation for why their fixes weren't holding.

Phase Two: Interpretation and Planning

The constraint hierarchy, validated from the suppression map, determines the intervention sequence for the 90-Day Plan. The Plan specifies which patterns are addressed in which order, which playbook actions are deployed in which weeks, who owns which actions, what the thirty-day milestones are, and how success is measured at Day 90.

The 90-Day Plan is not a project plan. It is a structural architecture document — a precise specification of what needs to change structurally, in what sequence, by when, and owned by whom.

The plan is presented to the leadership team in the PDI Debrief session — a structured ninety-minute conversation that opens with the founder's own language from the discovery conversation, moves through the suppression map, walks each pattern in canonical order, and closes with the proposed intervention sequence and its Doctrine rationale. This is the most skill-intensive session in the entire engagement, because it requires holding the intervention sequence under client pressure — which almost always comes.

The Implementation Dip

Every Business Alchemy™ engagement experiences a dip around weeks three to five. This is not a sign of program failure. It is a predictable structural phenomenon: the early structural investments have disrupted the existing stabilising patterns before new ones are established. The old patterns are no longer providing their stabilising function. The new structural architecture is in place but behaviours haven't locked in yet.

In this window, the business feels harder to run than it did before the engagement started. Leaders revert toward familiar behaviours. The founder's inclination is to step back into the operational centre. This is the moment at which most transformation programs are abandoned — not because they aren't working, but because they feel like they aren't working.

The implementation dip must be named explicitly and in advance. The week three conversation is: "In the next two weeks, this is going to feel harder before it feels easier. That's the structural disruption working. The moment you feel like abandoning the new structures is precisely the moment they most need to be held."

Phase Three: Execution and the Re-PDI

The ninety-day execution phase follows the constraint hierarchy established in the plan. Weekly review sessions maintain the accountability rhythm and surface real-time deviations from the intended sequence. The practitioner's primary function in this phase is not advice — it is constraint:

holding the Doctrine sequence when operational pressure generates the temptation to skip, accelerate, or reorder.

At Day 90, the PDI is re-administered. The comparative suppression map — the before and after picture of the business's structural pattern health — is the evidence base for evaluating progress and determining the next cycle's constraint hierarchy.

The re-PDI is not a graduation. It is the beginning of the next cycle. Pattern Science is not a one-time intervention. It is a structural operating discipline: the ongoing practice of diagnosing the current constraint, correcting it in sequence, and re-diagnosing the changed structural state.

Chapter Summary

- The 90-Day Alchemy Cycle follows three phases: Diagnostic (PDI + suppression map), Interpretation and Planning (constraint hierarchy + 90-Day Plan), and Execution (weekly review + re-PDI at Day 90).
- The implementation dip at weeks 3–5 is predictable and structural. It must be named in advance. The moment the founder wants to abandon the new structures is precisely the moment they most need to be held.
- The re-PDI at Day 90 determines the next cycle's constraint hierarchy. Pattern Science is not a one-time intervention — it is a structural operating discipline.

Chapter 13

Momentum and Enterprise Value

The compounding returns of structural alignment

Momentum in business is not a motivational state. It is not the feeling of progress, the energy of a team at its best, or the enthusiasm of a leadership group after an inspiring offsite. These are the subjective experiences of momentum. They are real and they matter.

But momentum, in the Pattern Science definition, is structural. It is the output generated by the sequential alignment of the five patterns through their three performance constructs. It is not a feeling that generates progress — it is a structural condition that generates progress regardless of how the team feels on any given day.

This distinction is the difference between momentum as a management aspiration and momentum as an engineering outcome. You cannot manage your way to motivational momentum. You can structure your way to structural momentum.

"Motivation creates momentum for a season. Structure creates momentum for a decade."

The Five Stages of Momentum Generation

Structural momentum builds through five sequential stages, each triggered by the structural conditions of the previous one. Understanding this sequence prevents the most common momentum management error: celebrating Stage 3 outcomes as though they were Stage 5 outcomes, then being surprised when the momentum doesn't sustain.

Stage One: Pattern Alignment

One or more patterns achieve Structural Coherence. The infrastructure is sound and correctly configured. This is the first structural condition for momentum — not its expression, but its prerequisite. At Stage 1, the business has the structural capacity for momentum. It has not yet generated it.

Stage Two: Behavioural Lock-in

The team's behaviours begin consistently reinforcing the structural architecture. People stop bypassing the system. Scorecards are completed without prompting. Meeting cadences are maintained under pressure. This is Behavioural Reinforcement rising to match Structural Coherence. At Stage 2, the structural architecture has genuine human support.

Stage Three: Outcome Consistency

Results begin to stabilise. Predictability increases. The business stops being surprised by its own performance. This is the stage that most businesses celebrate as the conclusion of transformation — and it is not. Stage 3 is structural stability, not momentum. It is the platform from which momentum can be generated, not momentum itself.

Stage Four: Momentum Emergence

Two or more adjacent patterns achieve Stages 1–3. The compounding effect of aligned patterns begins to express itself: results improve faster than effort increases. Growth begins to feel easier. New opportunities are noticed. The business attracts talent, clients, and capital more readily. This is the first genuine momentum stage — where the flywheel begins to turn.

Stage Five: The Flywheel

All five patterns achieve sufficient alignment. Momentum becomes self-reinforcing. Each pattern's performance strengthens adjacent patterns, which strengthens it further. Ownership liberates the founder. Clarity filters opportunity automatically. Rhythm sustains without enforcement. Flow attracts talent. Value multiplies margin. The business grows faster than the market. The founder is no longer operationally indispensable.

This is the structural condition that creates enterprise value that compounds — not as a consequence of the founder's continued involvement, but as a consequence of the structural architecture that operates independently of any individual.

The Momentum-to-Valuation Chain

The connection between structural momentum and enterprise value is not metaphorical. It is a direct, traceable causal chain that buyers, investors, and M&A advisors price, whether or not they articulate it in Pattern Science terms.

- Pattern Alignment generates Structural Coherence: the business's infrastructure is sound and self-sustaining across all five domains
- Structural Coherence produces Outcome Predictability: results become consistent and forecastable

- Outcome Predictability reduces Risk: a business with predictable, consistently achieved results carries significantly lower risk than a business of equivalent revenue with volatile performance
- Risk Reduction improves EBITDA Quality: not just the quantum of EBITDA but its sustainability, scalability, and independence from the founder
- EBITDA Quality drives Valuation Multiple: high-quality EBITDA commands premium multiples in M&A and investment markets
- Valuation Multiple creates Enterprise Value: the compounded output of structural pattern alignment, sustained through the flywheel

This chain is why Pattern Science is not a consulting methodology for operational improvement. It is a management discipline for enterprise value creation. Every intervention in the Business Alchemy™ architecture is designed to advance the business along this chain — from Structural Coherence through to the Valuation Multiple that reflects the quality of what has been built.

Chapter Summary

- Structural momentum is an engineering outcome, not a motivational state. It is generated by the sequential alignment of the five patterns.
- The five stages of momentum generation: Pattern Alignment, Behavioural Lock-in, Outcome Consistency, Momentum Emergence, and the Flywheel. Stage 3 is stability, not momentum.
- The Momentum-to-Valuation chain connects structural pattern alignment directly to enterprise value: Pattern Alignment to

Structural Coherence to Outcome Predictability to Risk Reduction to EBITDA Quality to Valuation Multiple to Enterprise Value.

Part Four
The Human Architecture

"You can build the most sophisticated structural system in the world. It will be operated by humans."

— Renae Fazakerley

Chapter 14

The NeuroTalent Method™

The behavioural intelligence layer of Pattern Science

This chapter is written by Renae Fazakerley, co-founder of Business Alchemy™ and creator of the NeuroTalent Method™.

When Troy and I began working together on what would become Business Alchemy™, we kept arriving at the same tension from different directions.

Troy was building the structural architecture — the pattern hierarchy, the constraint sequencing, the Interpretation Doctrine. He was mapping the invisible structural configurations that determine how businesses perform. His framework was rigorous, evidence-based, and structurally correct.

And then we'd sit in a client engagement and watch it hit the floor.

Not because the diagnosis was wrong. The diagnosis was always right. But because the structural correction was being handed to a human being — a specific human being with a specific behavioural architecture, specific motivational drivers, specific stress responses — and the structural plan hadn't accounted for that human being's pattern at all.

The founder who needed to hand over decision authority was a high-Stability type who had built her identity around being the team's support system. Handing over authority felt like abandonment. The structural plan was correct. It couldn't hold because the human implementing it hadn't been understood.

That's the gap the NeuroTalent Method™ was built to fill.

What the NeuroTalent Method™ Is

The NeuroTalent Method™ is a standalone methodology for high-impact recruitment and leadership profiling, built on the intersection of DISC behavioural science, NLP (Neuro-Linguistic Programming), and motivational psychology. Its foundational insight is that most recruitment and leadership development fails not because it misidentifies capability, but because it misunderstands motivation.

You can hire the right skills into the wrong behavioural environment and produce exactly the friction and underperformance you were trying to avoid. You can promote the right technical performer into a leadership role that is structurally incompatible with their motivational architecture and watch them fail — not because they lack intelligence or effort, but because the role demands that they operate against their nature in the domains that most determine success.

The NeuroTalent Method™ addresses this by mapping three layers of the human pattern:

- Behavioural Style: how a person naturally shows up — their pace, their communication approach, their response to conflict, their decision-making style
- Motivational Architecture: what drives them at an intrinsic level — the conditions under which they bring discretionary energy and the conditions under which they disengage

- Stress and Pressure Patterns: how they behave when conditions are difficult, deadline-driven, or ambiguous — which is when the gap between observed behaviour and true pattern most commonly widens

What the NeuroTalent Method™ Actually Measures

Most behavioural tools tell you how someone shows up. The NeuroTalent Method™ tells you why — and more importantly, what environment they need to show up at their best.

Renae built the method on a founding insight that twenty years of recruitment work confirmed: most hiring failures and leadership underperformance are not capability problems. They are architecture problems. The person has the skills. The environment doesn't fit the person. And no amount of coaching, feedback, or performance management changes that — because the mismatch is structural, not motivational.

The NeuroTalent Method™ assesses five dimensions of cognitive and behavioural architecture:

Processing Orientation

How a person naturally takes in and makes sense of information. Some people process sequentially and need complete information before deciding. Others process in patterns and move fast on incomplete data. Put a pattern processor in a role that demands sequential thoroughness and you get anxiety, cutting corners, or both. Put a sequential processor in a role that demands rapid intuitive decisions and you get paralysis.

Decision Sequencing Hierarchy

The order in which a person naturally weighs factors when making a decision. Some leaders lead with data, then people impact, then risk. Others lead with relationships, then gut instinct, then evidence. Neither sequence is superior. Both sequences in the same leadership meeting, without awareness of the difference, is the engine of most leadership team conflict that gets labelled a culture problem.

Pattern Recognition Mode

Whether a person naturally sees detail first or context first. Detail-first thinkers build precision and catch errors. Context-first thinkers build strategy and spot opportunity. A detail-first operator in a growth leadership role will slow the business down. A context-first operator in a compliance-heavy role will create risk. The role and the mode need to match.

Energy Allocation Curve

Where a person's discretionary energy naturally concentrates across the working day and working week, and what type of work generates versus depletes that energy. This is the dimension that predicts burnout before it happens — not by measuring stress levels, but by measuring the structural mismatch between energy architecture and role demands.

Adaptive Overlay Intensity

The degree to which a person is currently masking their natural behavioural architecture to meet perceived role expectations. High Adaptive Overlay means the person you see in the role is not the person who will show up under pressure, in conflict, or when the stakes are highest. It is the most important dimension in leadership assessment and the one that most behavioural tools miss entirely — because it requires understanding the gap between presented behaviour and natural architecture, not just measuring the presented behaviour.

The Friction Index™

Once the individual architecture is mapped, the NeuroTalent Method™ measures the Friction Index™ — the degree of structural mismatch between a person's architecture and their current environment across six domains: role fit, autonomy alignment, leadership congruence, cognitive pace compatibility, communication alignment, and reward structure fit.

Friction is not conflict. It is the invisible tax on performance that accumulates when a person's natural architecture is chronically misaligned with the environment they are operating in. A high Friction Index does not mean the person is wrong for the organisation. It means the structural conditions are generating resistance that no amount of motivation or management can overcome until the mismatch is addressed.

This is where the NeuroTalent Method™ connects directly to Pattern Science. Friction is the human expression of the same suppression logic that operates at the organisational pattern level. Just as a suppressed Flow pattern cannot express its potential because an upstream structural constraint is actively compressing it — a person with a high Friction Index cannot express their capability because their environment is structurally working against them.

You do not fix high Friction with coaching. You fix it by changing the structural conditions generating the friction. Sometimes that means changing the role. Sometimes it means changing the team structure. Sometimes it means changing what the role demands of the person. What it never means is asking the person to be different.

Where the NeuroTalent Method™ Integrates with Pattern Science

When the NeuroTalent Method™ is integrated into a Business Alchemy™ engagement, the leadership team stops being described in terms of personality and starts being described in terms of architecture. The question is no longer "why won't Sarah make decisions?" It becomes: Sarah's decision sequencing hierarchy leads with relationship impact — which means in a culture where decisions are made fast and alone, she will defer rather than decide. Change the decision-making environment and Sarah makes decisions.

That is the difference between a people problem and a structural problem. And it is the difference between a leadership development program that doesn't hold and a structural correction that does.

The integration points across the five patterns are specific:

- Ownership: before designing the accountability architecture, map the Adaptive Overlay Intensity of each leader — the gap between who they present as and who they actually are under pressure determines how each person needs to be supported to hold genuine ownership
- Clarity: the Strategic Message Cascade must account for Processing Orientation across the team — a context-first founder communicates strategy at a level of abstraction that a detail-first operator cannot execute against without translation
- Rhythm: the cadence design must account for Energy Allocation Curves — a daily standup that requires peak cognitive engagement at 7am is structurally incompatible with leaders whose energy architecture peaks mid-morning
- Flow: the Friction Index™ makes interpersonal friction structurally legible — what looks like a personality clash is

almost always a Decision Sequencing Hierarchy mismatch or a Cognitive Pace Compatibility gap

- Value: the Structural Misalignment Diagnostic™ identifies whether commercial underperformance is a skill deficit, role misplacement, authority suppression, overextension, or environmental incompatibility — each requiring a different structural response

The NeuroTalent Method™ in Recruitment

The standalone application of the NeuroTalent Method™ — outside of a Business Alchemy™ engagement — is in recruitment and leadership selection. This is where twenty years of specialist recruitment experience produces a methodology that most hiring processes cannot replicate: not the identification of technical capability (which most selection processes do reasonably well) but the prediction of performance and retention in the specific role, team, and culture context into which the person is being hired.

Most businesses hire for skills and fire for behaviour. The NeuroTalent Method™ profiles both before the hire, connecting the candidate's behavioural architecture to the specific demands of the role and the specific dynamics of the existing team. The result is a selection decision grounded in evidence about the human pattern, not just the technical qualification.

The NeuroTalent Method™ — Renae Fazakerley

The question I ask in every NeuroTalent assessment is not "is this person capable?" It's "in what environment will this person's capability actually show up?" Those are not the same question. And the answer to the second one is what determines whether a hire succeeds or fails.

Chapter Summary

- The NeuroTalent Method™ maps three layers of human pattern: Behavioural Style, Motivational Architecture, and Stress and Pressure Patterns.
- The four behavioural styles — Drive, Impact, Stability, Precision — each have natural alignments and risk points within the Business Alchemy™ pattern architecture.
- Structural pattern correction without behavioural architecture is a plan that doesn't account for the humans who have to operate inside it. The NeuroTalent Method™ is the human intelligence layer that makes structural correction durable.
- The NeuroTalent Method™ in recruitment addresses the most common hiring failure: selecting for capability without predicting whether that capability will actually express itself in the specific role and team context.

The Pattern Is Already There

The only question is whether you can see it

Every business described in this book — every construction company running a ninety-minute daily meeting that should be fifteen minutes, every founder carrying decisions that should be made two levels below them, every leadership team describing a culture problem that is actually a Rhythm deficit — has one thing in common.

The pattern generating those outcomes was always there. It was operating before the symptoms appeared. It will continue operating after the symptoms are treated, unless the pattern itself is changed.

This is the central claim of Pattern Science, and it is not a theoretical one. It is an empirical observation from twenty years of diagnostic work across hundreds of founder-led businesses. Chaos has a structure. The structure is composed of five interdependent patterns operating in a constraint hierarchy. The hierarchy can be diagnosed. The constraint can be identified. The correction can be sequenced.

And when it is — when the primary constraint is addressed first, when the behavioural architecture is aligned to the structural correction, when the sequence is maintained under the pressure of operational urgency and client impatience and the founder's own powerful inclination to move faster than the structure can support — the result is not just better performance.

The result is momentum. Structural momentum. The kind that compounds.

"Chaos isn't random. It's a pattern. And patterns can be changed."

— Pattern Science™

What Now – Three Pathways Forward

Readers of this book arrive from different places and are headed in different directions. The three pathways below are not mutually exclusive — many people begin on one and move to another — but they reflect the three most common starting points from which Pattern Science produces its most significant outcomes.

Pathway One: You Recognise Your Business

If you have read this book and found your business in its pages — if the Founder Bottleneck archetype described your leadership team, or the Strategic Chaos archetype named the pattern you've been calling "a priority problem" for two years, or the High BR / Low SC diagnostic trap explained exactly why your last consultant engagement didn't hold — then you already have the most important thing the Pattern Disruption Index™ will give you: the ability to see structurally.

The self-diagnostic in the previous chapter gave you an informal reading. The PDI makes it precise. It produces a suppression map, a constraint hierarchy, and an intervention sequence that removes the guesswork from what to fix first. More importantly, it gives you the structural language to have different conversations with your leadership team — conversations about pattern architecture rather than performance management, about structural correction rather than symptomatic treatment.

Pathway Two: You Recognise the Methodology

If you are reading this as someone who has spent a career inside businesses — seeing these patterns from the inside, watching interventions fail to hold, knowing that something deeper is generating the results no one can quite explain — and if the Interpretation Doctrine™, the suppression mapping process, and the constraint hierarchy feel like the architecture you've been working toward without knowing it had a name: Pattern Science™ is a methodology you can deliver.

The licensed practitioner programme is built for senior operators, executives, and advisors who have the credibility, the network, and the genuine disposition to hold the Doctrine sequence under client pressure. It is not a franchise. It is not a toolkit. It is a formally structured transfer of intellectual architecture — the methodology, the PDI, the playbooks, the Interpretation Doctrine — with the training, supervision, and governance required to deliver it at the level it demands.

The certification programme runs over eight weeks and covers the complete Pattern Science™ methodology: PDI administration and interpretation, suppression mapping, the five-pattern playbooks,

Interpretation Doctrine governance, client engagement management, and supervised practice delivery. Three certification levels: Associate Practitioner, Licensed Practitioner, and Master Practitioner. Each level unlocks additional delivery capability and commercial scope within the licensed network.

The practitioners who produce the most significant outcomes — for their clients and commercially for themselves — are the ones who have internalised the sequencing discipline, not just learned the framework. The Interpretation Doctrine™ is not a document you reference. It is a governance logic you apply without thinking, under pressure, when the client is pushing for the parallel action you know will produce a false recovery and regression.

That discipline is transferable. But it must be developed, not just taught. The practitioner programme is designed for that development.

Pathway Three: You Want to Go Deeper

If the theoretical foundations of Pattern Science™ — the General Systems Theory, the Theory of Constraints, the behavioural psychology research streams — have activated a desire to understand the intellectual architecture more fully before acting on it, the following resources will serve you well.

Eliyahu Goldratt's The Goal (1984) is the foundational text for constraint theory. It is written as a novel and reads faster than most business books. The manufacturing context can feel dated but the logical architecture is as precise and applicable today as it was when published. Read it for the Five Focusing Steps and for the intellectual rigour of what it means to identify the primary constraint before acting.

Peter Senge's The Fifth Discipline (1990) is the essential text for systems thinking applied to organisations. The concept of structural tension — the gap between the current state and the desired state generating the energy for change — maps directly to the Pattern Science suppression model. The sections on mental models and the learning organisation are particularly relevant to the Clarity and Ownership patterns.

Daniel Kahneman's Thinking, Fast and Slow (2011) provides the cognitive psychology foundation for understanding why founders and leaders systematically misread their own organisations. The availability heuristic, the narrative fallacy, and the focusing illusion all operate in the diagnostic errors that the Interpretation Doctrine™ is designed to prevent.

Edward Deci and Richard Ryan's work on Self-Determination Theory is most accessibly summarised in Daniel Pink's Drive (2009), which translates the academic research into the practical language of business motivation. The mapping of Autonomy, Competence, and Relatedness to the Ownership, Clarity, and Flow patterns is direct and practically illuminating.

A Final Note on Patience

Pattern Science is a discipline of patience in a world that sells urgency. The Interpretation Doctrine™ mandates sequencing when clients want parallel action. The constraint hierarchy requires that you begin where the structure demands, not where the pain is loudest. The implementation dip requires that you hold the line when everything in the system is pulling toward the old patterns.

This patience is not passive. It is the most active, disciplined, and consequential thing you can do with your understanding of how your business actually works.

The flywheel doesn't respond to force. It responds to aligned, sequenced, sustained structural investment. Apply it correctly and it turns. Once it turns, it turns faster. And the momentum it generates — the compounding structural momentum of a business whose five patterns are aligned — is the most commercially valuable thing a founder can build.

That is Business Alchemy™.

Troy Fazakerley

businessalchemy.au

info@businessalchemy.au

Acknowledgements

Business Alchemy™ was built in the field. The ideas in this book came from the businesses that trusted us with their most difficult structural problems — the founders who let us into the five o'clock meetings, who showed us the suppression maps before they had names for them, who held the Doctrine sequencing when everything was pulling them toward the familiar pattern.

To every client who has been part of this methodology's development: the framework in this book exists because of the courage you brought to the diagnostic conversations. Thank you.

To Renae: your contribution to Business Alchemy™ is not a chapter. It is the architecture that makes the structural work human. The NeuroTalent Method™ doesn't complement Pattern Science. It completes it.

This book was written with the assistance of artificial intelligence tools for research synthesis and manuscript development. Every idea, every field observation, every methodological claim, and every word of the Interpretation Doctrine™ is the product of twenty years of direct engagement. The AI helped organise it. The work was done in the field.

www.ingramcontent.com/pod-product-compliance
Lightning Source LLC
LaVergne TN
LVHW020643100826
845148LV00012B/2315

* 9 7 8 0 6 4 6 7 3 9 5 7 1 *